# Creating
# Inclusive
# Library
# Environments

# Creating Inclusive Library Environments

A planning guide for serving patrons with disabilities

**MICHELLE KOWALSKY**
**JOHN WOODRUFF**

An imprint of the American Library Association
CHICAGO / 2017

© 2017 by the American Library Association

Extensive effort has gone into ensuring the reliability of the information in this book; however, the publisher makes no warranty, express or implied, with respect to the material contained herein.

ISBNs
978-0-8389-1485-4 (paper)
978-0-8389-1487-8 (PDF)
978-0-8389-1488-5 (ePub)
978-0-8389-1489-2 (Kindle)

**Library of Congress Cataloging-in-Publication Data**

Names: Kowalsky, Michelle, author. | Woodruff, John, 1960- author.
Title: Creating inclusive library environments : a planning guide for serving patrons with disabilities / Michelle Kowalsky, John Woodruff.
Description: Chicago : ALA Editions, an imprint of the American Library Association, 2017. | Includes bibliographical references and index.
Identifiers: LCCN 2016026241| ISBN 9780838914854 (pbk. : alk. paper) | ISBN 9780838914878 (pdf) | ISBN 9780838914885 (epub) | ISBN 9780838914892 (kindle)
Subjects:  LCSH: Libraries and people with disabilities—United States.
Classification: LCC Z711.92.H3 K69 2016 | DDC 027.6/63—dc23 LC record available at https://lccn.loc.gov/2016026241

Cover images © Shutterstock, Inc. Book design by Kim Thornton in the Aleo, Vista Sans, and Expo Serif pro typefaces.

♾ This paper meets the requirements of ANSI/NISO Z39.48-1992 (Permanence of Paper).

Printed in the United States of America

21  20  19  18  17        5  4  3  2  1

# contents

# preface

**IT IS OUR INTENTION TO PROVIDE A ROAD MAP FOR LIBRARIES SO THAT** they may be proactive in creating inclusive library environments. As you review the accessibility of your library, this publication—and the discussions you have about it with others—will aid you in your quest to be truly inclusive.

## A Personal Note from John

Collaborating on this project intrigued me because it combined the issue to which I have dedicated my professional life—helping those with disabilities—with one of the resources I have ardently utilized throughout my life—the library.

Growing up, my frequent visits to our public library were prompted by both necessity and the pursuit of enjoyment. The need to utilize library resources for school projects was an absolute requirement. As one of nine children, I sought the many resources I needed, as well as the library's peace and quiet, which was also not available at home. When I was old enough, I would walk the mile to our town library and become happily lost in the books and magazines. I have always loved music, so it was a revelation to me that I could check out different types of media and listen to new artists in the days when my boyhood jobs did not provide enough discretionary income to purchase these items myself.

The library continued to be my one-stop destination for information and resources throughout high school and college. Each time I entered its doors, I crossed into another world and experienced a sense of calm. When the library began offering films to rent, it became my standard practice to stock up on movies for the weekend.

Those library trips eventually included my wife and children. It was a basic part of our routine to travel to the library together and then disperse to different areas of the building to investigate whatever sparked our interest on that particular day.

An important rite of passage for both my son and my daughter was to receive their first library cards. Even back then, I smiled when I remembered one of my professors in graduate school who would require that his children do research on the location of their upcoming family vacation. This also required use of a new library at their destination, an excellent excuse to practice their skills.

Which audio book to listen to on a family drive was always a highly debated subject. And sometimes, when we had a clear winner, we'd arrive at our destination still engrossed in the story and reluctant to leave the car.

Some of the joys I still have to this day are to enter a library, to browse what is new, to see what peaks my interest, and to recall why I went to the library in the first place. I'm sure I'm not alone in this experience. Many users visit the library with a particular goal in mind. Once that goal is achieved, they may stay longer because they have consciously or unconsciously given themselves permission to linger among the books, journals, magazines, or movies.

My professional life has focused on championing the rights of individuals with disabilities and helping businesses and organizations understand these rights. This project seemed a natural fit, considering my vocation for disability resources and my love and respect for the many services offered by libraries.

## A Personal Note from Michelle

I too escaped to the library anytime being at home got boring or tedious. I rode my small, red ten-speed bicycle to the only two places I was allowed—the libraries on either side of town. It was my freedom! Even as a teenager I was clearly more out of shape than John, because a 1.5 mile ride each way tired me out for the rest of the night. I'm pretty sure everyone at home actually liked it that way.

Riding eastward on the side of the road, through a slow series of traffic lights in the commercial part of downtown, I ended up at my local public library. I had just moved into town, and suddenly I needed sources for a research report for school. I was directed to the children's room as a fifth grader, but quickly exhausted the nonfiction offerings there. It was suddenly official—I was no longer a child, and the library was my proof.

Once I had the official green reciprocal borrowing sticker on my adult library card—which at the time seemed more valuable than real money—I branched out. I rode my bike westward instead, down a flat and straight but busy suburban street, to the public library of the town next door. Here I stuffed books, music, and fliers into yellow plastic bags like a crazed supermarket checker. I then attempted to ride home (never in a straight line) with the bags in one hand and handlebars in the other. It's a wonder I never got run over.

As an adult, I absolutely never ride my bike and I don't miss it one bit. But I still love my library card and I still entertain myself—after working all day in a library, mind you—by going to the public library . . . any and all, near, and far. If you are accompanying me at any time, you may also be asked to take my photo in front of the nearest library sign, so consider yourself forewarned.

I guess I never really knew much about disabilities until I started teaching more than twenty years ago. My K–12 students had physical or learning disabilities, often accompanied by second-language challenges and personality disorders. Until then, the people with disabilities that I had encountered were patrons of the public library, customers at the supermarket, or neighbors. Suddenly it became my professional responsibility to understand them, and that was when my learning curve really accelerated.

As I grew older, my own family began to include members who have such disabilities as autism spectrum disorders, blindness, genetic and developmental disorders, physical disabilities, early-onset dementia, and speech-language impairments. While it was unusual at first to encounter these conditions because they had not been common in my family, dealing with the challenges of disabilities became a normal part of life.

I have learned from personal experience that advocacy turned into action is indeed the best way we can support others. When you truly understand, your actions speak a special kind of language that communicates your respect, empathy, and love all at once.

## Format of this Book

This book provides the reader with an easy-to-use guide to valuable strategies and resources related to disability and access issues that are specifically related to libraries. In each chapter we will explore a variety of themes and highlight best practices recommended for libraries to follow in order to create a more inclusive and barrier-free environment. Resources at the end of each chapter point to additional information on each topic.

## Acknowledgments

The authors would like to thank Jamie Santoro, our acquisitions editor at ALA Editions, for her optimism and support of our work throughout this process. The authors would also like to thank those colleagues who provided feedback on drafts of this monograph: Maureen Woodruff, Thomas Edison State University; Carol Roth, Imperatore Library, Dwight-Englewood School; Bryna Coonin, Joyner Library, East Carolina University; John W. Adamus, Rutgers, The State University of New Jersey, New Brunswick; and Bruce Whitham, Rowan University.

# CHAPTER 1

# Introduction to Creating Inclusive Libraries

EFFECTIVE EDUCATORS, LIBRARIANS, AND MANY OTHER ADVO-cates help to create inclusive environments on a daily basis. We hope this book will help you continue to learn new ways to reach and teach others.

Sometimes those we teach are in elementary, middle, and high schools. At other times, we work with young adults in college, or adults who may be raising families and participating in the workforce, or retirees in our local communities. A great many more users will defy these traditional categories, in as many ways as there are individuals. Yet as we meet all of these unique and valuable people, we naturally come to realize that all share the same needs—to understand and to be understood.

Libraries can connect people with mentors, role models, and new ideas that fuel their growth. Many times, library staff members can take on leader-

## *i* For Your Information

We can all identify a mentor who helped us understand or learn something new about the world or about ourselves. These dedicated educators helped us navigate the world by

- Modeling appropriate behavior, and correcting us when necessary.
- Sharing information, advice, or perspective to help us see new things.
- Remaining unwavering in their encouragement of our growth.

**For Your Information**

As we take what we have learned from mentors and apply it to our own lives, we are able to help others by

- Participating in our communities, organizations, and institutions, in order to ensure that educational opportunities exist for everyone.
- Teaching, administering, counseling, and supporting our users within various institutions, from our local universities to our global multinational companies.
- Remaining unwavering in our commitment to improving our society.

ship roles in addressing issues of disability within their communities. Since information resources help us to develop as humans in complex relationships, as well as to appreciate the development of others, libraries easily become a source of lifelong learning for everyone.

By engaging with an individual and establishing rapport, a mentor is able to evaluate the level of need, to establish a frame of reference for the relationship, and to provide resources for further learning. Library staff members therefore become natural educators and mentors who are able to meet and greet users, to determine their level of interest and skill, and to help them decide where to start navigating the library or refining their information needs. These mentoring skills are invaluable in creating relationships with all types of patrons, and in sustaining these relationships over time.

Librarians and users alike share a certain kinship within the library environment. Whether helping or being helped, library users report that these relationships usually result in a positive library experience when each user's needs are met. Libraries that encourage the development of these human and information resources are indeed leaders in creating welcoming environments for further education and gainful employment, the cornerstones of self-sufficiency and independence that we all have come to expect as members of a democratic society.

This book is in honor of all of you who shared your expertise with us through your excellent library service, your presentation and teaching, or your writing. Please continue to share so that we all may continue to learn.

## The Americans with Disabilities Act at Twenty-Five

The Americans with Disabilities Act (ADA) defines a disability as a mental or physical condition that causes a substantial limitation. This definition is significantly restricted as to the condition, manner, or duration when compared to the condition, manner, or duration under which the average person in the general population can perform any major life activity.

It has been more than twenty-five years since the ADA became law in 1990. With the passage of the ADA, significant progress was made in the physical accessibility of buildings and all public places such as restaurants and libraries. Libraries became accessible in many more ways, from parking spaces to sidewalks, curb cuts, ramps, and automatic doors leading into the buildings. It is also more common for indoor furnishings and facilities to comply. Library desks, tables, and bathrooms are made to be fully accessible to accommodate persons with physical disabilities. Most elevators and doors have Braille signage for those with visual impairments. And online access to library holdings, as well as software and hardware that help to achieve this, have been evolving ever since.

Years before the ADA was signed in to law, many champions of the disability-rights movement laid the groundwork for improving access for persons with disabilities. Remembering their courage, sacrifices, and determination helps us to create and maintain a world in which today's heroes encourage everyday acts of tolerance, acceptance, and kindness.

## The ADAAA of 2008

Eighteen years after the ADA went into effect, the Americans with Disabilities Act Amendments Act (ADAAA) was signed into law in 2008. The catalyst for

 **For Your Information**

So who is considered to be an individual with a disability under the ADA? A person who

- Has a physical or mental impairment that substantially limits one or more of his or her major life activities.
- Has a record of such an impairment.
- Is regarded as having such an impairment.

the new legislation was the need to get closer to the original intent of the law. The ADAAA made important changes to the definition of the term "disability" by rejecting the claims in several Supreme Court decisions and clarifying portions of the previous ADA regulations of the US Equal Employment Opportunity Commission (EEOC).

These changes made it easier for individuals seeking protection under the ADA to qualify as eligible for accommodations due to a disability within the definition provided by the ADA. EEOC's "Fact Sheet of Final Regulations Implementing the ADAAA" was published in the *Federal Register* in 2011, and now appears online at www.eeoc.gov/laws/regulations/adaaa_fact_sheet.cfm. It has become the go-to document for explaining these changes.

Furthermore, the ADAAA emphasizes that the definition of disability should be construed in favor of broad coverage of individuals to the maximum extent permitted by the terms of the ADA, and generally should not require extensive analysis. One of the significant changes that resulted from the ADAAA is that it left open the interpretation of who would qualify as having a "disability."

For example, an individual with a history of cancer who is currently in remission would be covered under the new regulations. Another key change made it easier for individuals to establish coverage under ADAAA specifically within the "regarded as" part of the definition of "disability." These changes also affected who might qualify as eligible for reasonable accommodations on the job or in places of public accommodation.

## Overview of Barrier-Free Strategies

When an environment like a library, a classroom, or a retail shop is said to be barrier-free, it is easily negotiated by everyone, including those who have disabilities. In other words, no special actions on the part of the person with a disability are needed in order to use, experience, or engage in any aspect of that environment. Specifically, when nothing in particular keeps any person from accessing a resource, service, or place, those places can be described as "barrier-free" or by similar terms like "accessible" or "universally designed."

Accessibility relates to minimizing the differences between persons with and without disabilities who engage with the library environment. Library buildings should be showcases of accessible public spaces via careful design

> ✅ **Checklist**
>
> Start the conversation about accommodating disabilities in your library:
>
> - ☐ Determine your organization's background knowledge of abilities and disabilities.
> - ☐ Identify a plan for facilities that includes new and existing functions.
> - ☐ Review policies and procedures that identify relevant actions and activities.

and upgrade of their structure and interiors. Many libraries have updated furniture, equipment, and entryways in recent years, and there are many exciting examples of reimagined and newly designed spaces in libraries, schools, and other places. A great number of libraries have already implemented book shelving that is wide enough to accommodate electric wheelchairs, or have redesigned service desks so that their surfaces are now more comfortable for patrons who must remain seated. While these major improvements are often visible to even the most casual library users, examining the subtler aspects of your library facility may also reveal new opportunities and strategies for upgrades. For example, additional adjustments to the physical environment of the library might include more sensitive controls for lighting, noise, or air flow. Mechanical room-darkening shades may not only help an audience see a Microsoft PowerPoint presentation more clearly, but may also help to influence the behavior of children with disabilities during story times.

Classical music, played through strategically located speakers, which can be directed to or removed from a particular area of the library, might create a relaxing atmosphere and simultaneously help to soothe the nerves of restless teenagers. Specific facility improvements and options are explored further in chapter 3, Setting Up Facilities.

Policies and procedures are essential in creating a barrier-free library environment, and they must cover many types of situations. On college campuses, for example, students with service animals are required to register with the office of disability resources. Usually, service animals are permitted in such places such as the college residence halls, the cafeteria, classrooms, and of course the library. However, some users may bring animals that do not qualify as service animals into a public, school, or special library, so policies must be in place to help govern these actions. In addition, users are also not required to

**For Your Information**

The US Department of Labor reminds us that, when communicating with people who have disabilities, we should

- Relax.
- Treat the individual with dignity, respect, and courtesy.
- Listen to the individual.
- Offer assistance, but do not insist or be offended if your offer is not accepted.

register their animals in advance of entering any other place of public accommodation, further complicating staff decision making about the best courses of action. Therefore, the many details of library policies must be discussed and put into place to govern the behavior of library users as well as that of library staff, which is the focus of chapter 2, Writing Policies and Procedures.

By conducting your own research in library sources, and considering your experiences and those of knowledgeable colleagues or experts, you will be able to begin thinking about developing materials that help others to learn about accessibility. For example, the staff of the Disability Resources Center at Rowan University created fact sheets to distribute to our employees that describe the most common physical and invisible disabilities among our particular community of users, which currently include auditory processing disorders, post-traumatic stress disorders, traumatic brain injuries, and hearing and visual impairments.

Fact sheets like these can be created by your own organization and customized for your particular needs. They may be used as resources for training and disability-awareness sessions, along with other training materials for new employees or for refresher sessions for returning employees. Links to organizations and videos for further information can also be provided to serve as companion resources for teachers and support staff. These disability fact sheets can be invaluable in heightening awareness of specific disabilities and best practices to support and understand individuals in the classroom and to provide full access to their educational experiences. Information on these and other types of strategies for service improvements are addressed in chapter 4, Training Library Staff.

Sometimes library staff may not always know what type of help a library user might want, and must also realize that sometimes users explicitly don't

> ## ✅ Checklist
>
> To prepare for effective library operations:
> - ☐ Explicitly train staff by demonstrating effective interactions.
> - ☐ Address negative perceptions and misconceptions early and often.
> - ☐ Empower both employees and library users to make appropriate decisions.

want help. For example, an elderly person staring at the large-print fiction shelf for a long time might unwittingly prompt a staff member to interrupt his browsing like a retail worker at the mall trying to interact with a shopper. Not every patron action demands a reaction from library staff.

The staff member might not realize that a user is just fine, and may be reading slowly because she forgot her glasses or has dyslexia, not because she does not know how to use the library. Similarly, there may be other reasons that a user may be looking at the shelf for a long while, or pausing in a seemingly frozen position before reaching from his wheelchair for an item. It may be that he just can't decide whether he is interested in historical fiction or if he has already read the fourth James Patterson novel, not because he has mobility issues. Again, sensitivity is key.

Because persons with disabilities interact with libraries on a daily basis, it is important that library staff have the training necessary to feel confident and comfortable providing assistance. One way to promote effective communications and positive interactions with persons with disabilities would be to use recommended first-person language. Determining the appropriate language to use in advance of meeting users with disabilities will ensure that staff members are addressing, assisting, and accommodating each user in an appropriate manner. To provide the reader with strategies for communicating with persons with disabilities, user engagement is explored further in chapter 5, Maintaining Daily Operations.

Libraries are often the central hub where students gather to study or users visit to do research or to check out specific resources for later study. For this reason, the library environment presents an ideal opportunity to showcase disability-related themes throughout the year.

An example of outreach might be a partnership with an institution for incarcerated youth or a workshop sponsored by the local health clinic. When we think of the disenfranchised, we often may not remember that people with disabilities may also be members of this group. Staff members from other institutions are usually very receptive to activities, programs, and outreach that meet mutual goals.

Alternately, suggesting general ways to work together and specific projects (with details of whom might be involved) are excellent opportunities to widen the library's impact. More ideas on how to involve others in removing barriers for people with disabilities are elaborated in chapter 6, Collaboration and Outreach.

Another way in which libraries can be advocates in creating inclusive environments would be to host events and speakers during themed months throughout the year. Library staff can design workshops, programming opportunities, open houses, and tours of the library that explicitly highlight new assistive technologies, tips, or resources available to persons with disabilities.

Professional conferences and publications provide opportunities to identify possible speakers and trainers, although library staff members and community users will also have significant expertise in many potential topics for workshops. Additional suggestions for events and showcase activities are provided in chapter 7, Programming and Workshop Ideas.

In order to serve the many users who do not set foot in a library building, accessible web pages and accessible information literary tutorials are essential. Many academic and public library websites make digital access easier by having obvious links at the top of their home pages that lead to the most-requested resources. Such design features can save valuable time when navigat-

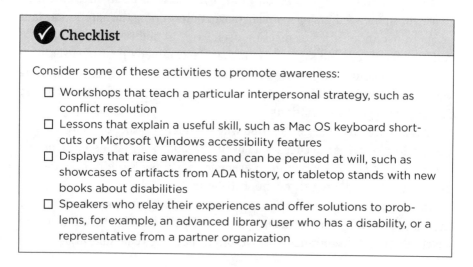

✔ **Checklist**

Consider some of these activities to promote awareness:

☐ Workshops that teach a particular interpersonal strategy, such as conflict resolution

☐ Lessons that explain a useful skill, such as Mac OS keyboard shortcuts or Microsoft Windows accessibility features

☐ Displays that raise awareness and can be perused at will, such as showcases of artifacts from ADA history, or tabletop stands with new books about disabilities

☐ Speakers who relay their experiences and offer solutions to problems, for example, an advanced library user who has a disability, or a representative from a partner organization

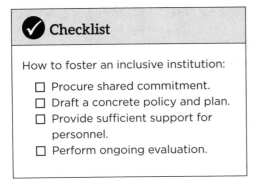

**✓ Checklist**

How to foster an inclusive institution:

- ☐ Procure shared commitment.
- ☐ Draft a concrete policy and plan.
- ☐ Provide sufficient support for personnel.
- ☐ Perform ongoing evaluation.

ing the website and will greatly increase repeat visits for digital access to library materials.

Some libraries also have opportunities to become the primary location for students with disabilities to check out adaptive equipment and assistive technology when convenient, often because of their longer hours of operation. These items are available in a central location, and assistance for using both new and traditional types of equipment is available. More ideas for offering accessible options can be found in chapter 8, Accessible Resources and Technologies.

Libraries can become advocates in creating inclusive environments through programming opportunities, open houses, and tours of the library that highlight new assistive technology and resources available to persons with disabilities. Simultaneously, library culture must be infused with new strategic plans related to improving strategies that encode empathy and action into the organizational culture.

Developing new traditions, adjusting the language we use in person and in writing, and improving the spaces in which we provide our materials and services are ways in which libraries can ensure that their brands are inclusive. By examining, maintaining, and strategically influencing the beliefs and behaviors of the organization, the library is able to affect the tone and tenor of its entire community. For more ideas on how to effect strategic change, see chapter 9, Developing a User-Centered Culture.

Keeping current is a vitally important aspect of librarianship, and a necessity for all educators. Reading about emerging technologies and trends, and experiencing a variety of specific resources and technologies, will aid you and your library in advocating for persons with disabilities. Similarly, seeking out current research and applying its recommendations will help ensure that you are implementing best practices, and not just acting on the opinions of others. Maintaining contact with those at other libraries and other types of organizations that serve people with disabilities will help to broaden your awareness of available information. In "How to Foster an Inclusive Institution," for example, the Association of Research Libraries (1994) reminds us of steps we could take every day. Ways to find these ideas and more are addressed in chapter 10, Keeping Up to Date.

The everyday needs of library users vary greatly. Therefore, the design of inclusive library environments is essential to meet the diverse needs of all library users, not just those identified as having a disability. Inclusiveness goes beyond a best practice or universal design. It is a welcoming atmosphere that keeps users coming back because of a positive experience and excellent customer service in addition to the access of limitless library resources.

## Libraries as Employers

Libraries are not the only institutions trying to identify ways to accommodate users with disabilities. Corporations, government offices, professional organizations, and many types of institutions are also seeking ways to comply with federal regulations. Furthermore, in addition to serving people with disabilities, libraries of all types employ people with disabilities. Libraries will act as a resource to provide other employers and employees with information on this topic.

Consider the case of Hal Godwin from Philadelphia Electric Company (PECO), who many consider to be one of the pioneers in the area of disability awareness training in his community. Hal served on the Philadelphia Committee for the Employment of Persons with Disabilities. As a young engineer, Hal—a wheelchair user—was the first individual with a severe disability hired by PECO. According to Hal, he was called by Human Resources to schedule his interview. The day he arrived for his interview, he had no way to access the building. Not to be deterred, Hal recruited two volunteers to carry him and his wheelchair up the steps and into the building to meet his interviewer.

Hal was hired. In addition to a successful career with PECO, he was considered an advocacy champion because of his commitment to working to raise disability awareness of employers throughout Pennsylvania. After his retirement from PECO, Hal was honored as a Top Pennsylvanian by the Pennsylvania Governor's Committee on the Employment of Persons with Disabilities in recognition of his commitment to promoting the value of employing persons with disabilities.

Hal's involvement with the Pennsylvania Office of Vocational Rehabilitation as a Windmills trainer was one example of his commitment to chang-

**For Your Information**

Using the clever acronym ADEPT, Pimentel's (2001) strategy provided a roadmap for preparation of your workplace for people with disabilities:

- A—Anticipate barriers, problems, and employer concerns.
- D—Develop solutions and strategies.
- E—Educate participants to present themselves effectively to the employer.
- P—Prepare the employer to work efficiently with people with disabilities.
- T—Transition the job seeker into a successful employee through retention strategies.

ing the attitudes of employers and promoting disability awareness in hiring practices among employers in the region. Windmills, developed by Richard Pimentel, was a disability awareness training program popular in the 1980s. The program provided employers with a full week of materials to immerse their employees in simulations of having disabilities. For example, employers could spend a day or more in a wheelchair, or blindfolded to simulate being visually impaired. The Windmills training model was used by many government agencies, and large and small companies as well as employer organizations.

Pimentel is seen as one of the early champions of the disability-rights movement. In addition to creating his disability training program Tilting at Windmills, he authored *Working with People with Disabilities in a Job Placement/Job Retention Environment*, which offered both employers and job developers practical advice and strategies for communicating with, and preparing their workplace for, new employees with disabilities.

Libraries are in a unique position to model for other organizations the appropriate systems and processes for employing persons with disabilities. And when and if we fail to provide appropriate services, accommodations, or communication, this feedback helps us determine what additional information would be needed to help others avoid our mistakes. In developing collections that reflect the best practices of our society, and in trying to follow those practices on a daily basis, libraries can become beacons of equity in their communities.

## Universal Design

In creating a more inclusive library environment, it becomes essential to employ universal design principles because they are a cornerstone in ensuring equal access for all users. Universal design, a concept and term widely used today, was first coined by Ronald L. Mace, an architect with North Carolina State University. Also referred to as "inclusive design," it takes a look at all environments, such as buildings and products, as items that should be designed with all types of people in mind—young and old, with and without disabilities.

---

 **For Your Information**

The 7 Principles of universal design from North Carolina State University's Center for Universal Design (2014):

**Principle 1: Equitable Use**
The design works for everyone, resulting in the same type of use, outcome, or benefits without alienating any particular group or individual.

**Principle 2: Flexibility in Use**
The design allows for individual preferences, customization, or options to be set by the user.

**Principle 3: Simple and Intuitive Use**
The design is obviously understandable by all, at any given time, and for any given skill level.

**Principle 4: Perceptible Information**
The design itself helps people know how to use the item or service, and does not require additional explanations, directions, or training in order to understand or participate.

**Principle 5: Tolerance for Error**
The design is a result of advance troubleshooting, and has minimized the number of things that could go wrong during use.

**Principle 6: Low Physical Effort**
The design promotes efficiency, comfort, and ease of use by everyone.

**Principle 7: Size and Space for Approach and Use**
The design accommodates users of all shapes and sizes, in an appropriately sized space.

According to the Center for Universal Design in North Carolina State University, these principles can be applied to existing items like building features or furniture or websites, can guide the design process for upgrades of these items and for new products or services which are yet to be offered, and can serve to educate designers and consumers about ways to make their innovations more easily usable by more people. The purpose of the principles is to guide the design of environments, products, and communications as a natural and global standard for literally everyone and everything.

## Physical Access

Title II of the Americans with Disabilities Act developed standards for the design of new construction and communicated expectations for modifying or retrofitting existing buildings. Known as ADAAG (Americans with Disabilities Act Architectural Guidelines), this document provided clear instructions for architects and builders to follow when designing physical access points for public buildings.

Twenty years later, the Department of Justice amended the Title II regulations, which led to the 2010 ADA Standards for Accessible Design. These revised standards went into effect in 2011 and looked at seven areas: Element by Element Safe Harbor, Ticketing, Service Animals, Wheelchairs and Other Power-Driven Mobility Devices, Effective Communication, Residential Housing Offered for Sale to Individual Owners, and Detention and Correctional Facilities. However, exceptions were provided to existing buildings which had been previously modified after the ADA went into effect in 1990. For example, a ramp designed for new construction would follow the amended regulations of 2010. Yet it is conceivable that the existing buildings nearby may have ramps with steeper grades that met the design standards at the time of their construction.

Renovations are an excellent way for libraries to show true understanding of the ADA that goes beyond simply bringing structures up to code. For example, the University of California at Berkeley has undertaken many significant renovations in recent years, and its library website provides a comprehensive list of resources and links to ADA construction guides.

The age and original architectural design of a library would determine if any modifications are necessary to improve physical access and create a more inclusive space. When making modifications or embarking on new construction, it is important to seek input from key stakeholders. Users, consultants, and professionals specializing in accessible design who are knowledgeable about the ADA guidelines for existing and new construction are often readily available.

## Digital Access

Improving digital access and web accessibility continues to be a critical area where an organization needs to make an ongoing commitment in reviewing its websites using Web Content Accessibility Guidelines (WCAG). Viewing your library website through the perspective of a user with a disability will ensure that your web pages are all accessible to individuals who are blind or have visual impairments.

Accessibility is a shared responsibility, delegated to everyone in an organization whose role involves writing, designing, or posting content on a website. Content would include any web applications, which including code, text, images, video, and sound. So it is important to assign responsibility to several staff members to check websites against the WCAG standards because it is truly in everyone's best interest to understand how the organization's website meets current criteria and to identify areas for improvement. Because the content on any organization's website remains fluid, it makes sense to train as many employees within the organization as possible to reference the WCAG guidelines at all stages of web design, including the ongoing monitoring and updating of pages on the library website, and monitoring new pages provided by third parties.

The recommendations of the Web Content Accessibility Guidelines Working Group (WCAG WG), World Wide Web Consortium (W3C), and Web Accessibility Initiative (WAI) set the standard for modern accessible web design. WCAG 2.0 guidelines are organized under four principles: they must be perceivable, operable, understandable, and robust.

Web pages must provide textual descriptions for any photographic content and captions for any video content, which enable the content to be converted into other formats like large print, Braille, speech, symbols, or simpler language. Web designers can also organize website content in different ways, including simple layouts and menus, so that no content is embedded in or communicated solely by structure, color, or graphic design. It is important to choose a design that will work for multiple current and future devices.

Also construct navigation of your library website in a way that allows for keyboard-only operation, and include skip-navigation options and breadcrumb-style pointers to help users determine any item's location within the structure of your website. A predictable structure will help minimize user error and frustration. Also, avoid color and flicker schemes that do not add value to the content. In other words, communicate your content logically, make it easy to read, and ensure it is easily understood by everyone.

An increasing number of students and faculty and staff with disabilities are here, prompting our recognition of both visible and hidden disabilities. Persons with these challenges are searching for digital access to books, alternate textbook formats, journal articles to browse, and much more. Therefore, we must bring our libraries up to speed regarding modern digital access methods.

Digital access is not just an accommodation or necessity for persons with visual impairments. For example, individuals may have a print disability, or they may simply be auditory learners who learn best by having their digital books read to them via use of screen readers, which maximizes their retention of material. Technological enhancements such as this can help everyone, not just people with disabilities.

Today, most—if not all—computers have accessibility features that are easy to activate and customize to the personal preference of the user. There are also a growing number of free screen readers that can be downloaded to provide audio access to whatever content may be on the screen of any computer, tablet, or mobile device. So, whether browsing the Internet or listening to a textbook for class or a book for leisure, the availability of assistive technologies is essential to ensure digital access for persons with disabilities.

## Consulting Existing Library Resources

Libraries are staffed with helpful and well-trained professionals ready to assist users in connecting with resources, books, journals, movies, and much more. So, with a goal of creating more inclusive library environments, it is essential to look at existing library resources for more information on how to do this. Below are a few examples to get started in researching this topic.

The University of Washington DO-IT publication "Equal Access: Universal Design of Libraries," written by Sheryl Burgstahler (2012), is an excellent universal design model for libraries that is easy to follow. Its resource checklist for making libraries welcoming, accessible, and usable is comprehensive and covers legal issues, universal design, and guidelines, and provides a section on the planning, policies, and evaluation of services offered by the library.

The Center for Universal Design in Education (CUDE) at the University of Washington combines Principles of Universal Design and Universal Design for Learning and Instruction to create strategies for applying universal design to educational products and activities. Located in the DO-IT Center, the website provides a multitude of resources for designing accessible learning environments.

Visit the Great Lakes ADA Center website, which lists three model programs for universal design as well as additional resources. The models include the Center for Universal Design (CUD) at North Carolina State University, mentioned earlier as the genesis for the 7 Principles of Universal Design, along with the Idea Center at the University of Buffalo, and The Institute for Human Centered Design (IHCD) in Boston.

The Association of Research Libraries (ARL) has an Accessibility and Universal Design Working Group that addresses these types of concerns as well. The group facilitates a blog entitled "Web Accessibility in Research Libraries," which is an enhancement of ARL's Web Accessibility Toolkit. Specifically, its blog promotes digital inclusion and connects research libraries with the tools, people, and examples they need to provide accessible digital content.

A Web Accessibility Toolkit by Dr. Jonathan Lazar of Towson University in Maryland is offered as online or in-person training. Professor Lazar's home page also provides a formula for institutions working on increasing accessibility, as well as many videos and articles that can be used for training or self-study.

The Association of Specialized and Cooperative Library Agencies (ASCLA) has a useful toolkit of information called "Library Accessibility—What You Need to Know." This professional group provides web resources along with online webinars and professional committees to assist with questions and answers about library services for special-needs populations.

By being proactive, a library can have resources such as these readily accessible to the community by posting the information in optimal locations inside the library, on their websites and social media, and with other partner organizations.

There is another particular resource that everyone seems to forget—the human resources of our staff, our professional colleagues, and our own library patrons. We've all learned about disabilities (and about libraries, for that matter) from another person, personal experience, or some circumstance. In hearing others' stories, we are able to integrate new information into our own experiences and increase our sensitivity to the experiences of others.

The authors are no different; we each have had experiences that led us to internalize best practices, or to recognize and troubleshoot problems, or to feel some of the daily struggles of those unlike ourselves. Our own growth has intensified over time, and is a direct result of others—including people with and without disabilities—who have shared their knowledge with us.

Next, the authors each provide a bit of context about their work that has helped to inform their thinking about disabilities and inclusive environments.

## John's Experiences: A Disabilities Coordinator Learns about Libraries

I first entered the field of disability rehabilitation, awareness, and training in 1983 as a twenty-three-year-old college graduate, eager to embark on a meaningful career. I spent the next twenty-four years assisting persons with disabilities to become gainfully employed and training them to do their jobs despite their physical or mental limits. The last decade has been spent helping college students with disabilities access the resources they need in their pursuit of college degrees.

I was fortunate to work with AHEDD, a highly regarded nonprofit human resource organization. Founded in 1977, AHEDD continues to be a cutting-edge organization that champions equal access to employment and career opportunities for persons with disabilities entering or returning to the workforce. I had the charge of overseeing the operations throughout Southeastern Pennsylvania.

Many of my early mentors from AHEDD who influenced and shaped my career were forward thinking individuals and pioneers in the field of rehabilitation and employment of persons with disabilities. AHEDD—whose mission is to be "a catalyst in the employment and training of persons with disabilities"—continues to thrive, because it stays true to a basic and proven tenet that hiring a person with a disability is a good business decision.

During my years at AHEDD, I interviewed, hired, and trained many employment specialists. Early in the training process, I would often make arrangements to meet the new employment specialist at a local library in the town or region that would be eventually be his territory. In turn, when scheduling meetings with AHEDD participants with disabilities, the library was the preferred location.

The library environment was always rich with welcoming staff members who were informative and helpful in locating a wealth of resources for the job seeker with a disability. In addition, the library itself became an ideal site to secure volunteer opportunities for job seekers with disabilities, especially those lacking any work experience. The relationships established with local libraries were usually long-lasting and afforded numerous persons with disabilities valuable unpaid work experience.

Once a volunteer moved on to a paid position outside the library, additional opportunities for persons with disabilities opened up. The next employment specialist or job coach would often accompany the volunteer with a disability to ensure a smooth transition into the library environment and to help the volunteer become familiar with her duties and responsibilities.

These volunteer opportunities resulted in mutually beneficial learning experiences for the library staff and individuals with various disabilities. As a result, the positive impact an inclusive library could have on library patrons and staff—as well as on the community at large—was truly amazing. An inclusive and welcoming environment opens the door for endless possibilities for many kinds of collaborations.

Individuals with disabilities may need additional resources to put them on equal footing with other workers, but they also possess diligence and tenacity that makes them valuable employees who are able to make a contribution to any organization they join.

## Michelle's Experiences:
## A Librarian Learns about Disabilities

In one of my first professional teaching jobs, I worked with students who were learning English as a second language. I had been formally trained in linguistics and instructional methods for language learning, reading, and writing, so I figured this would be pretty easy for a native speaker.

But I had no idea that that these students could have learning disabilities in combination with other challenges. Some of them buckled under the heavy cognitive load associated with attending classes taught in a foreign language. Others became frustrated at the extra time it took to navigate a computer keyboard or when they encountered a website for the first time. And that wasn't counting all of their adolescent social issues!

Very quickly I needed to figure out ways to help these students learn all the skills they needed in order to participate in class and school activities. This proved especially challenging when most of the students were starting out at very different places cognitively, linguistically, and emotionally. We laughed and we cried, and we epically failed at times, but we all resolved to never give up.

During my twenty years as a K–12 classroom teacher and school librarian, I realized that I had been given an incredible opportunity to learn about the many available solutions and aids for providing equitable learning environments and materials for students and faculty with disabilities.

My regular library customers were students with limited wheelchair mobility due to multiple sclerosis, or students with emotional disorders who were prone to surprise outbursts, or students with blindness from birth who required multiple technologies just to keep up with their peers. It was my job to provide them with the content and format of instruction they each needed, and I absolutely had to deliver.

I recall becoming best friends with many special education teachers, guidance counselors, disciplinarians, learning disabilities consultants, school psychologists, and physical education teachers. My favorite collaboration was with a Braille transcriptionist; together, we literally and figuratively plotted ways to make raised biology and chemistry diagrams with limited supplies, and attempted to troubleshoot the embossing printer right before class handouts were needed. These were partnerships forged in a climate of trust, kindness, social justice, and equity. Together we helped to double-check each other's assumptions and then to teach others how to act—through modeling, corrective feedback, and appreciation of our students and fellow educators.

We always knew this task would be never-ending, because discrimination is experienced daily by those we served. If any of our assistance made their paths a bit easier to travel, then every effort and every little win along the way was—and continues to be—entirely worthwhile.

## Our Current Educational Context

The authors both currently work at Rowan University, a comprehensive public university in the state university system of New Jersey. Recently designated as a research institution after the addition of two medical schools, Rowan University was formerly a four-year state college with a proud history of preparing future teachers.

Campbell Library, a 130,000-square-foot building in the center of our suburban campus, houses computer labs, library book stacks, classrooms, office spaces, and group-study rooms. The building next door, Savitz Hall, now provides centralized student services from varied departments such as the Academic Success Center, Tutoring and Testing, Disability Resources, Veterans' Affairs, Student Housing, and more.

The Campbell Library has an array of resources for students, which include the Digital Scholarship Center and The Writing Center, along with large- and small-group spaces for classroom and library instruction. Library tours are conducted for new and transfer students, and signage throughout the library highlights the services and resources available.

The Digital Scholarship Center on the third floor of the Campbell Library is a truly inclusive space with a universal design that is frequented by users with and without disabilities. As a technology learning area, it is equipped with Macs, PCs, lounge-style seating, and a variety of peripherals like large-format printers, piano keyboards, and scanners. This welcoming space is routinely used for training sessions during Disability Awareness Week on campus and throughout the year. It contains designated computers equipped with assistive technology such as JAWS and Kurzweil 3000 for users with visual impairments and print disabilities. Separate studio rooms may also be reserved for distraction-reduced study. A high-speed scanner and a CCTV for users with visual impairments complement the resources available to all users.

By providing accessible spaces and services, libraries become excellent partners for other organizations, departments, or programs. For example, on Rowan University's campus, the Campbell Library collaborates with the Office of Disability Resources and Office of Veterans' Affairs to display items and books in their glass showcases in October for Disability Awareness Week; in November during Veterans' Week; and in April during Autism Awareness Month.

This partnership also resulted in a community-wide event in the library to celebrate the twenty-fifth anniversary of the Americans with Disabilities Act.

> **✅ Checklist**
>
> Ways to create accessible learning spaces:
> - ☐ Provide comfortable furniture that can be moved, removed, or adjusted.
> - ☐ Purchase appropriate computing devices including computers, keyboards/mice, software.
> - ☐ Train staff members to assist users as needed.

In addition, these existing partnerships led to a new collaboration with the Office of Social Justice, Inclusion, and Conflict Resolution, in which librarians and Disabilities Resources staff members participated in the development of training for new members of our university campus.

University libraries have the added benefit of providing group-study rooms and other spaces for students studying together, many of whom spend countless hours in the library doing homework or project research and utilizing the many available resources and services. In fact, the Campbell Library's expanded hours of operation during the academic year make it the one building on campus open late for students. During finals week, Campbell Library is open around-the-clock and offers coffee and other refreshments.

Libraries in our local area have also influenced our outlook. The Bucks County Library System in southeast Pennsylvania is a good example of a library system with a progressive website that is effective in providing essential information about locations, resources, research, events, downloads, and streaming. At their many branches, libraries provide friendly and warm environments for information seeking, thinking, reflection, and participation for people of all abilities.

Another excellent example of a library that provides increased access for persons with disabilities is the New Jersey State Library Talking Book and Braille Center (TBBC) located in Trenton, NJ. TBBC is a network library of the National Library Service for the Blind and Physically Handicapped (NLS), a division of the Library of Congress. TBBC serves New Jersey residents whose ability to read is affected by physical impairment, reading disability, or vision impairment. Its responsive staff provides resources and collaboration throughout the state. An online search of the NLS website will help you find similar services in your state or region.

Inclusive libraries are neither a fad nor a pipe dream; they are tangible, sincere reflections of our belief that equity in access is a fundamental human right. By striving to implement the ideas in this book, your library will become a more reflective organization, and your staff a more agile response team. Just as in other areas of librarianship, sharing of information and collaboration are key components that can make every library an inclusive one.

## Resources

AHEDD: A Specialized Human Resource Organization. www.ahedd.org.

Association of Research Libraries. 2014. "How to Foster an Inclusive Institution." accessibility.arl.org/how-to-become-accessible/.

Association of Specialized and Cooperative Library Agencies. 2015. "Library Accessibility—What You Need to Know." www.ala.org/ascla/asclaprotools/ accessibilitytipsheets.

Bucks County Library System. "Bucks County Free Library Branches and System Member Libraries." buckslib.org/locations.

Burgstahler, Sheryl. 2015. "Universal Design of Instruction (UDI): Definition, Principles, Guidelines, and Examples." Disabilities, Opportunities, Internet-working, and Technology (DO-IT) Center, University of Washington. www.washington.edu/doit/universal-design-instruction-udi-definition -principles-guidelines-and-examples.

Center for Universal Design in Education, University of Washington. "Overview." www.washington.edu/doit/programs/center-universal-design-education/ overview.

Great Lakes ADA Center. 2015. "Celebrate 25 Years of the Americans with Disabili-ties Act." May 8. www.adagreatlakes.com/Resources/Default.asp?category=29.

Lazar, Jonathan. 2015. "Homepage of Dr. Jonathan Lazar." triton.towson.edu/ ~jlazar/.

The Library of Congress. "That All May Read . . . National Library Service for the Blind and Physically Handicapped (NLS)." www.loc.gov/nls.

National Disability Authority (NDA), Centre for Excellence in Universal Design (CEUD). 2014. "What is Universal Design: The 7 Principles." www.universal design.ie/What-is-Universal-Design/The-7-Principles.

New Jersey State Library. "Talking Book and Braille Center." www.njstatelib.org/talking-book-braille-center.

North Carolina State University. Center for Universal Design. 2008. "Universal Design Principles: Resource Page." www.ncsu.edu/ncsu/design/cud/about_ud/udresourcepage.htm.

Organization for Autism Research. Schwallie Family Foundation and Global Regional Asperger Support Program. 2008. "Understanding Asperger Syndrome: A Professor's Guide." www.youtube.com/watch?v=233-3jtEZck.

Pimentel, Richard. "The Art of Disclosing Your Disability." Milt Wright and Associates, Inc. www.miltwright.com/articles/artofdisclosingyourdisability.pdf.

Pimentel, Richard, and Milt Wright and Associates. 2001. *Working with People with Disabilities in a Job Placement/Job Retention Environment.* Northridge, CA: Milt Wright and Associates.

Psychiatric Service Dog Partners. 2015. "[Service Dog] Work and Task List." www.psychdogpartners.org/resources/work-tasks/work-task-list.

Rowan University. www.rowan.edu/home.

Rowan University. Academic Success Center and Disability Resources, Glassboro Campus. www.rowan.edu/studentaffairs/asc/disabilityresources.

Rowan University. Campbell Library, Glassboro Campus. www.lib.rowan.edu/campbell.

Sisson, Patrick. 2015. "The ADA at 25: How One Law Helped Usher in an Age of Accessible Design." www.curbed.com/archives/2015/07/23/how-the-americans-with-disabilities-act-transformed-architecture.php.

United States Access Board. 2002. "ADA Accessibility Guidelines (ADAAG)." www.access-board.gov/guidelines-and-standards/buildings-and-sites/about-the-ada-standards/background/adaag.

United States Department of Justice. Civil Rights Division. "Fact Sheet: Highlights of the Final Rule to Amend the Department of Justice's Regulation Implementing Title III of the ADA." www.ada.gov/2010_regs.htm.

————."Information and Technical Assistance on the Americans with Disabilities Act: ADA Standards for Accessible Design." www.ada.gov/2010ADAstandards_index.htm.

————. "Information and Technical Assistance on the Americans with Disabilities Act: State and Local Governments (Title II)." www.ada.gov/ada_title_II.htm.

United States Department of Labor. Office of Disability Employment Policy. 2002. "Communicating with and about People with Disabilities."www.sabeusa.org/wp-content/uploads/2014/02/Communicating-With-and-About-People-with-Disabilities.pdf.

United States Equal Employment Opportunity Commission. "The Americans with Disabilities Act Amendments Act of 2008." www.eeoc.gov/laws/statutes/adaaa_info.cfm.

———. "Fact Sheet on the EEOC's Final Regulations Implementing the ADAAA." www.eeoc.gov/laws/regulations/adaaa_fact_sheet.cfm.

———. 2011. "Regulations to Implement the Equal Employment Provisions of the Americans with Disabilities Act, as Amended." *Federal Register,* March 25. www.federalregister.gov/articles/2011/03/25/2011-6056/regulations-to-implement-the-equal-employment-provisions-of-the-americans-with-disabilities-act-as.

University of California, Berkeley. 2016. "Construction and Design Guide: ADA and Universal Design." guides.lib.berkeley.edu/construction/ada.

University of Montana. "Faculty Course Preparation Guide." www.umt.edu/accessibility/getstarted/faculty.php.

University of Washington. Disabilities, Opportunities, Internetworking, and Technology (DO-IT) Center. 2015. "Universal Access: Making Library Resources Accessible to People with Disabilities." www.washington.edu/doit/universal-access-making-library-resources-accessible-people-disabilities.

Web Content Accessibility Guidelines Working Group (WCAG). 2012. "Web Content Accessibility Guidelines Overview." October 2. www.w3.org/WAI/intro/wcag.

Wentz, Brian, Paul T. Jaeger, and Jonathan Lazar. 2011. "Retrofitting Accessibility: The Legal Inequality of After-the-Fact Online Access for Persons with Disabilities in the United States." *First Monday* 16, (11). journals.uic.edu/ojs/index.php/fm/article/view/3666.

# CHAPTER 2

# Writing Policies and Procedures

THIS CHAPTER WILL REVIEW COMPONENTS OF BASIC LIBRARY policies, including ADA compliance, rules for behavior in the library, and statements of accommodation for service and comfort animals, for proper use of equipment, and the like.

Getting to know your patrons is probably the best way to determine what policies and procedures your library will need. As our fiduciary responsibility, protecting users' rights to privacy and confidentiality should be a priority when drafting or revising any library policies. Likewise, we must also protect the organization by maintaining reasonable yet compliant policies that are understandable to our users.

Most of the time, your library will be in a position to revise existing policies to take into account new ADA standards and guidelines. Sometimes you will need an entirely new policy to address an issue that had not come up previously, such as one relating to a new technology or trend.

The best policies are broad enough to take into account these minor shifts in technology or user and staff behaviors. Sometimes the policies are strong but staff members' enforcement of them is weak, or users' requests for changes to them are relentless. In either case, checks on the effectiveness and currency of library policies and procedures will help to provide the best possible experience for our patrons.

It will be tempting to include the particular details of problems you have encountered in order to help provide some leverage for enforcement in written policies or signage. In fact, it is often quite funny to enter an unfamiliar library and see signs posted everywhere advertising that library's problems! This should not be your default mechanism for either notification or education; rather, it may be an indication that there is some lack of alignment between your policy and its enforcement, or between your policy and the needs of its users, or even its management.

Librarians can use both free and licensed library resources to research a policy topic, including (but not limited to) samples of other libraries' policy wording. Take the time to look through all of the relevant primary sources, not just the ones that are convenient or familiar, for guidance in your decision making about policy wording.

Policies will give staff at every level a roadmap for delivering services in all areas of the library. Well-written policy delegates authority for enforcement to staff members at every rank by helping them clearly articulate the reasons for, and nature of, any library policy on the books.

 **For Your Information**

The US Department of Agriculture provides sample policies and considerations for many types of organizations that write policies, and its guidelines easily cross-apply to libraries:

- Policy decisions will affect the well-being of the entire library.
- Policies can be broad and general or detailed and specific.
- Broad policies leave room for interpretations and the exercise of judgment and initiative.
- Policies should deal with a recognized need, and should be the result of careful thought and research.
- Policies should be reviewed for internal bias by an outside reviewer.
- Policies must not conflict with any other library policies, bylaws, laws, etc.
- Policies should deal with recurring practical situations, and clearly indicate the conditions, to whom, and to what extent they apply.
- All policies are not equally important. Some policies are of such importance they determine the character of the organization. Others are limited in scope and could be changed or eliminated without significant impact.
- A well-written and constructed policy mediates differences between conflicting values.

**For Your Information**

The Association of Specialized and Cooperative Library Agencies (ASCLA) Tip Sheets explain what librarians, administrators, and trustees need to know about disabilities in libraries and policies in the areas of

- Assistive technology
- Autism spectrum disorders
- Children with disabilities
- Deaf and hard of hearing
- Developmental disabilities
- Learning disabilities
- Management
- Mental illness
- Multiple disabilities
- Physical disabilities
- Service animals
- Staff
- Vision
- Volunteers with disabilities
- What trustees need to know

Policies exist for every area of library service, although some may be unwritten and merely habits of past practice. Try to articulate—perhaps in a staff manual—what the usual procedures are, and how those processes relate to library policies. While patrons may not need handbooks detailing how procedures are implemented, each policy should be worded clearly enough to suggest a course of action that is both logical and appropriate.

For example, your circulation system may be set to block borrowing when a user has twenty items checked out. Is this truly your current and standard practice? Does it correspond to the spirit of your written and approved circulation policy? Is the number of checkouts arbitrary, or just "the way we've always done it"? Are your policies and your practices flexible enough to allow for an exception? If so, who will determine if exceptions be made, and under what circumstances?

Library policies are meant to communicate transparently the rules of how the library operates to both users and staff members. Sometimes, they are meant to help control unusual behaviors or to document appropriate responses to unusual requests. In every instance, however, they should demonstrate the values of libraries and reflect equity of use by all.

## Periodic Review of Existing Policies

Of course, it is necessary to update your existing policies to use modern language and reflect current best practices. Do any of your policies still mention a card catalog, or discuss "the handicapped," or include procedures that really are not policies? Then it is definitely time to review your existing documents. Inspect your library's policies for old wording and approve new policy language accordingly. A helpful online resource is available on New York State's Office for People with Developmental Disabilities website. Its web page has a list of outdated terms used to describe persons with disabilities and gives their modern equivalents. The extensive list was compiled by the Institute for Community Inclusion, which modified original material created by the Mid-Hudson Library System Outreach Services Department of Poughkeepsie, New York. A portion of this list is reprinted here.

Policies are a reflection of the philosophy and values of your library, and of libraries everywhere. It would be useful if each policy helps the library to achieve a specific objective related to sharing, respect, equity, diversity, or responsibility. Thus, you would be able to determine why certain policies are required, and justify why they must be communicated to everyone.

*Collection policies* improve our services to our users; *environmental and behavioral conduct policies* improve interactions between users, as well as staff; and *online and website policies* ensure that all authorized users are able to use all of the materials available to them. If any of your policies lack terms that ensure equity of access or First Amendment rights, these items can be added easily. Many examples from peer libraries are available.

Sometimes certain policies may also indicate a process for dispute (i.e., materials challenges) or a time line for responding to requests (i.e., interlibrary loan or room reservation activities). They may indeed be distinct from a how-to list of directions for initiating a book challenge, for borrowing a book from interlibrary loan, or for reserving a room for an outside event.

---

### ✅ Checklist

Does your library have these collection-related policies?

- ☐ Borrowing
- ☐ Collection management
- ☐ Book challenge/removal requests
- ☐ Fines and replacement of materials
- ☐ Donations
- ☐ Copyright
- ☐ Request for purchase

# General Guidelines

| OUTDATED OR OFFENSIVE TERM: | REASON(S): | CURRENT TERM: |
| --- | --- | --- |
| "The" anything:<br>The blind<br>The autistic | Views people in terms of their disability; groups people into one undifferentiated category.<br>Condescending; does not reflect the individuality, equality, or dignity of people with disabilities. | - People with disabilities<br>- People who are blind<br>- People with autism |
| Handicapped | Outdated; connotes that people with disabilities need charity.<br>Disabilities don't handicap; attitudes and architecture handicap. | - People with disabilities |
| The disabled | An individual is a person before one is disabled; people with disabilities are individuals who share a common condition. | - People with disabilities |
| Admits she/he has a disability | Disability is not something people admit to or that needs to be admitted to. | - Says she/he has a disability |
| Normal, healthy, whole | People with disabilities may also be normal, healthy, and whole. | - Non-disabled |
| Normal, when speaking about people without disabilities as compared to people with disabilities | Implies that the person with a disability isn't normal. | - Person without a disability |
| Courageous | Implies person has courage because of having a disability. | - Has overcome his/her disability<br>- Successful, productive |

From New York State's Office for People with Developmental Disabilities, www.opwdd.ny.gov/sites/default/files/documents/communitylink_welcome_guide_0.pdf.

Library policies should explain the philosophy behind providing these services, and give clear, unshakeable guidelines on how they should be executed. This means that policies should neither be too specific nor too general (which will lead to enforcement problems), and they should be neither too prescriptive nor too relaxed ( which will lead to interpretation problems). Ideally, staff members should know what the policies do, and understand how to enforce them, just by reading them.

## Words, Connotations, and Diplomacy

Your policy statements should clearly link aspects of the library's vision with the services and resources you provide. Policies will often be invoked when some aspect of your daily operation is questioned by a user, or some problem occurs that puts two users at odds, or some situation is used against a staff member. In a best-case scenario, your policy would describe what is done and why, leaving no ambiguity about its logic or rationale.

If you need to explain further why a rule exists or to whom it applies, this means that your policy is too wordy or convoluted for staff members to learn by heart. Some words in your policies may trigger anger, agitation, or eye-rolling; these loaded words should be replaced by more neutral ones so that the delivery does not overshadow the message.

An organization is totally within its rights to set rules for its customers and employees. These rules should be based on a fundamental philosophy or belief about why the organization exists, and policies should always flow clearly from this place of good faith.

A policy should be written in words that help employees make good decisions within the parameters given, and which should also help managers spend their time managing problems and not managing individuals or daily interactions. Words should be unambiguous, resulting in a nearly identical interpretation by all. When consistent and fair treatment is the goal of a policy, as well as the reason it is enforced, everyone's needs are met and fewer problems arise.

The wording of policies should help provide a sense of guidance for your community. Policies help users understand that the environment will be consistently maintained and that they will be treated the same every time, barring any change in policy (which they should be informed of promptly, and in advance whenever possible).

> **✓ Checklist**
>
> Here are some guidelines for writing policy documents. Whenever possible, use
>
> - [ ] Active, action verbs
> - [ ] Present tense
> - [ ] The same terms to define the same items or services across policies
> - [ ] Third-person language instead of second-person language to avoid directing rules at the reader ("you must have your library card")
> - [ ] Shorter, direct sentences without subordinate clauses to avoid statements that are conditional ("if this happens")
> - [ ] A professional, rather than a conversational, tone

If possible, especially during revisions, structure each subsequent policy in a similar manner. Every policy's beginning, middle, and end should unfold in the same way. Use the same types of headings, numbering and outline features, and section lengths and breaks.

Simple terms without multiple connotations are usually best, and those used to indicate persons with disabilities are no exception. Use a subject and a strong verb in your sentences, choosing the simplest word over the more literary one, while avoiding generic terms that could mean just about anything. For example, "patrons must register at the children's reference desk for all children's programs" (a formal policy) is more effective than "parents should go to the desk to sign your child up for programs" (a conversational procedure).

Not all policy stakeholders will be skilled writers, so first work on the document as a group to solidify the content, then allow one or two members to polish the grammar and sentence structure later. The document should sound consistent in tone and word choice as if it was spoken by one person, rather than like a compilation of individual statements by special interest groups.

It may be tempting to discard previous versions of policy statements, but their revision history is useful for legal reasons. It's fine to define new or unfamiliar terms until these concepts take hold in society or your community. However, choosing your terms carefully should eliminate the need to revise frequently, but still take into account many eventualities of the present and near future.

## Incorporating Evolving Best Practices

Some policies may seem sudden, too innovative, or unusual when we first encounter them. Imagine how we all reacted when barcodes, passwords, and wireless hotspots were first introduced! At the time, they may have seemed too new to need policies, too unusual to understand, or even too niche or fleeting to garner attention in a formal document. Now, many of those original and innovative ideas are normal parts of our work. And new ideas will eventually replace them, at an ever-quickening pace. This does not mean that the policy should change for every new eventuality; a strong policy should already encompass most types of events in the major categories of service.

For example, you may already have a policy about pets or smoking in your library. Specific mentions of service or comfort animals may already be included in the existing policy. If not, modifications can be made easily without revising the entire document. If your library has routine issues with a particular topic, for which the current policy seems not to hold, perhaps a more expanded policy is needed.

However, sometimes it is the enforcement of a policy that is the real problem, and not the policy itself. This can be discerned by logging the number and type of incidents that are not addressed in a satisfactory manner over the course of a semester or year. Recurring violations may suggest better or more consistent enforcement, especially if they come from the same users. Policies should ideally provide guidelines about what gets enforced, and they should address the most important aspects of the library's business.

ADA guidelines specify that the appropriate size and space will be provided for approach, reach, manipulation, and use of any library equipment and furniture, regardless of a user's body size, posture, or mobility. Although this

### ✔ Checklist

Does your library have these facility-related policies for the following?
- ☐ Filming and photographing
- ☐ Room reservations and use
- ☐ Patron conduct and responsibilities
- ☐ Acceptable computer use
- ☐ Public accommodations laws

may not be specified in any policy, procedure, or signage, it may be practiced automatically behind the scenes by library staff members who recommend and make purchases. Some rules are actually state or federal laws, which may not need to be restated as library policies.

Daily practices may not be written down anywhere, yet they may be commonly accepted rules that guide decisions. Making this type of information more explicit to staff members, especially new ones, would help individuals share their knowledge about ADA recommendations with the entire organization. This would illustrate that all decisions are not made solely because of ADA rules, but rather are informed by ADA concerns.

## Technology Access Policies

Your library's technology policies are probably the items that might need more frequent revision than the others. As Internet processes become more complex, so do access, privacy, and confidentiality issues.

Sometimes operational aspects of your technological processes will change, but seldom will require a modification of your technology policy. For example, requiring chip-enabled library cards for Internet logins may be an update of a card-swipe or other login system used previously at your library. If your tech policy is well-written, its parameters will already encompass this new system and simply speak to the essential rules of who may use library computers and how to access them.

Physical access to library spaces, and use of the contents of these spaces, likely need policies as well. For example, the New Jersey Library Association suggests language for describing meeting-room spaces that not only affirms

---

### ✅ Checklist

Does your library have these technology-related policies?
- ☐ Acceptable use and inappropriate access
- ☐ Public computer time limits
- ☐ Personal and information safety
- ☐ Respect for equipment and bandwidth
- ☐ Confidentiality and privacy

the library as a public space but also ensures that facility policies are in line with the library's mission. Applying a fair policy consistently will ensure that it neither caters to any particular group nor excludes another.

However, if you find that a new gaming or popular online social networking service requires users to circumvent your existing security policies, information may need to be added to your policy if no statement is already present about purposefully or inadvertently altering the library's network security. Wording that instructs users to adhere to existing laws of federal, state, and local government will remind them of the criminal and civil penalties for such acts.

Users with disabilities are often frequent customers of your library's technological resources, so policies that espouse equity of access and use will be especially important for them. Accessible workstations are not only for users with disabilities. Because they are modified for ease of use, and ideally, universally designed for comfort, they benefit all users.

Policies that affirm each individual's constitutional rights—and which identify ways to resolve issues when two or more individuals' rights come into conflict—will be useful guides when a problem arises.

The easiest way to determine effective wording for technology policies is to look for samples from other libraries. The peer institutions you investigate should be ones that are known to provide extensive technology for patron use, and/or have high numbers of active users. This will help to identify policies that have been able to withstand a variety and volume of uses.

## Behavior and Activity Policies

Predictability, consistency, and safety are probably the most important aspects of library special events planning and production, as well as daily operations. The neurodiversity of potential attendees, along with the spectrum of physical disabilities in the general public, requires a bit of planning in order to ensure an equally enjoyable experience for all.

One example of appropriate language in action can be seen in the Anythink Library System in Colorado, whose librarians presented on this topic at the Public Libraries Association (PLA) conference recently. Library staff members are trained in first-person language as well as in appropriate ways to uphold

> ✓ **Checklist**
>
> Does your library have these behavior-related policies?
> - ☐ Unattended children
> - ☐ Patron code of conduct
> - ☐ Smoking, eating, drinking, etc.
> - ☐ Cell phone or audio use
> - ☐ Obscene, abusive language or behavior

existing policies and educate users about them. The policies themselves use appropriate terminology to avoid offending any particular group.

Using policy and practice to build relationships with people with disabilities made Anythink's staff more comfortable with all types of interactions. As a result, its programs for persons with disabilities became more robust. Users and their caregivers knew what to expect, and library staff knew how to interact with users in ways that were comfortable, predictable, and kind.

Other librarians around the country are excellent sources of further information on the synergy between policy and practice. At a recent workshop, Renee Grassi, Youth Department Director of the Glen Ellyn Public Library, and Holly Jin, Community Engagement Supervisor of the Skokie Public Library, both of Illinois, provided some additional tips to help librarians provide disability-friendly customer service.

Some of these included practices and policies for utilizing visual supports, for participation in sensory story times, and for accessible tours and walk-throughs of the library building. Regular communication about the policies, and the activities they permit and encourage, will make coming into the library a less stressful task for those who wish to participate.

Information about how to ask questions about policies will also help those who have concerns about these issues and the way they should be handled. Interaction with patrons should include giving clear questions and directions, offering choices for action and reaction, and allowing time to process what you have said.

Adjust your delivery and communication during policy situations on a case-by-case basis. Have handy any print copies or the web addresses of the complete texts of library policies, which will help everyone communicate more easily. Questions about policies do not necessarily turn into arguments as long as there is a process in place for both informal conversation (venting about experiences) and formal disagreement (registering a challenge).

## Special Collections Policies

Archives and special collections staff members should be able to recognize a disability and be able to render requested assistance or refer the patron to another source of help such as the reference desk or even another type of institution, as needed.

Accommodations should be provided unless they pose undue hardship on the organization. Patrons should be familiar with the type and extent of help available in advance, via a policy statement on the web page of the collection or parent organization. Libraries must strive to avoid situations that might result in unequal treatment of users, such as withholding original documents from those with physical disabilities or roping off an exhibit area that includes a ramp.

An important concept to emphasize to staff is that users are entitled to find, review, and communicate information without mediation from other people who are sighted, hearing, or ambulatory. Researchers should be able to search, find, browse, and discover at their own pace and in their preferred sequence. Sometimes, knowing in advance about these freedoms will instantly attract new users, especially if they are able to find a web page, brochure, or audio description of the particular services, facilities, assistive technology, and accessible collections that interest them.

Making these pages easy to locate will increase interest in the library's collections and promote efficient use by those who visit. If a problem occurs, the professionalism of staff will demonstrate that they are responding to the inquiry seriously, courteously, and diplomatically.

## Involving Key Stakeholders in Policymaking

A natural component of your policymaking strategy should be to involve those whom the policies would affect most. These include users, employees, and those who oversee any part of the process. Stakeholders should come from all aspects of your library's user community, including young and old, newbies and experts, and, of course, users with and without disabilities.

The stakeholders should include more than "just one young person" or "just one person in a wheelchair," which will ensure the needs of all constituencies are represented. A variety of stakeholders can comment and advise, while others can be designated to carry the messages to a round-table discussion.

Some strategy groups may make the mistake of combining all disabilities into one category. This may occur if negotiations are not transparent or if decisions are made too quickly. Just as we would not group all new arrivals to our country into a single category by assuming speakers of diverse languages and cultures to be automatically similar, disabilities are not easily categorized either. It is important not to generalize user characteristics.

Inviting stakeholders with disabilities to serve on a planning or policy revision committee may also require forethought, because many of those who could contribute the most detailed information may not be able to do so in a traditional conference room or by speaking at a whole-group meeting.

Allow a sufficient amount of lead time for users with disabilities to learn about the planning process and then contribute their comments via telephone, live Internet chat or video, or prepare physical accommodations or asynchronous options during a longer meeting. Participants may want to prepare and submit their written comments in advance, or would prefer to be interviewed by a committee member who would then recount their comments and concerns to the group. This is especially helpful for users with disabilities who want their identity to remain confidential or anonymous.

---

## ✔ Checklist

Invite these stakeholders to participate in brainstorming and decision making:

- ☐ Library patrons from multiple stakeholder groups
    - Children's services
    - Young adult services
    - Adult services
- ☐ Library employees
- ☐ Library administrators
- ☐ Representatives of other/related community offices
- ☐ Special collections donors
- ☐ Board members
- ☐ Local or parent organizations
- ☐ Library legal counsel

Many stakeholders will be library users or staffers, but others may be experts in the field of disabilities or in the field of law. Disability advocates in your community can provide professional advice on policy making to complement the experiential advice provided by caretakers or other concerned citizens.

The "squeaky wheels" may volunteer to serve as committee representatives—in other words, those who complain the loudest or are the most upset with a particular policy may want to be more involved in the process. Similarly, overly complimentary or agreeable representatives should not dominate policy conversations. Honest, objective dialogue seems to work best to produce a quality product.

Some libraries may not have access to objective professionals who can advise on matters of disability advocacy or law. In this case, some research in books and journals can go a long way to prepare your library's response to potential issues and problems. Professional organizations often have free speaker services as well.

 **For Your Information**

Ways to help users and staff become more familiar with library policies include:

- Providing the text of the policy on your library web page, with its approval date and authority clearly indicated.
- Giving the URL of the policy's location in a newsletter or social media post, with a short summary of its contents and/or notes about changes or updates.
- Writing and circulating a short scenario (i.e., a social story) about a problem and how its corresponding policy would be enforced in the library by a staff member.
- Hold a role-playing event, puppet show, or training session (as appropriate for different audiences). Create videos of these with the appropriate informed consents.
- Encourage users to report violations directly to staff members rather than handle it themselves; provide table tents, sticker arrows, or verbal reminders to continually direct users back to staff members for assistance.
- Use critical friends as "secret shoppers" to spot-check how staff members respond to difficult inquiries. (Warning participants in advance might help to reduce the stress of being judged.)

While no library is immune to lawsuits, much information is available about how to prevent and deal with them. It is worthwhile to consult a lawyer specializing in disability law either before embarking on policy revision or after new policies have been drafted so that a targeted discussion can take place. Many additional suggestions from vetted professionals are easily researched.

"Privacy and Confidentiality Issues: A Guide for Libraries and their Lawyers," by Sarah McHone-Chase, a lawyer from the Freedom to Read Foundation, is an example of information written specifically for library staff. First Amendment questions, constitutional rights, and privacy concerns are all addressed, along with examples of court cases and how to defend against them.

And naturally, remember to lay out plans to distribute your policies and procedures in accessible formats. Planning for the dissemination of policies, especially new ones, is just as important as creating them. Some libraries may want to publicly list the names of the representatives on a policy revision committee, or even include contact information for an administrator who can answer questions about the policies. In most circumstances, increased transparency will reduce suspicion about how the library operates.

## Resources

American Library Association. 2016. "Libraries and the Internet Toolkit: Access for People with Disabilities." www.ala.org/advocacy/intfreedom/iftoolkits/litoolkit/accessforpeoplewithdisabilities.

———. 2016. "Outreach Resources for Services to People with Disabilities." www.ala.org/advocacy/diversity/outreachtounderservedpopulations/servicespeopledisabilities.

———. 2009. "Services to Persons with Disabilities: An Interpretation of the Library Bill of Rights." www.ala.org/advocacy/intfreedom/librarybill/interpretations/servicespeopledisabilities.

American Library Associaiton. Association of Specialized and Cooperative Library Agencies. 2010. "Accessibility for Patrons with Service or Support Animals: What You Need to Know: Library Accessibility Tip Sheet 8." www.ala.org/ascla/sites/ala.org.ascla/files/content/asclaprotools/accessibilitytipsheets/tipsheets/8-Service_and_Suppor.pdf.

———. Association of Specialized and Cooperative Library Agencies. "ADA and Libraries." www.ala.org/tools/ada-and-libraries.

American Library Association. Intellectual Freedom Committee. 2016. "Questions and Answers on Privacy and Confidentiality." www.ala.org/advocacy/intfreedom/librarybill/interpretations/qa-privacy.

Anythink Library System. Rangeview Library District, CO. www.anythinklibraries.org.

Association of Research Libraries. 2012. *Code of Best Practices in Fair Use for Academic and Research Libraries*. Association of Research Libraries. www.cmsimpact.org/sites/default/files/documents/code_of_best_practices_in_fair_use_for_arl_final.pdf.

Bonnici, Laurie J., Stephanie L. Maatta, Jackie Brodsky, and Jennifer Elaine Steele. 2015. "Second National Accessibility Survey: Librarians, Patrons, and Disabilities." *New Library World,* 116 (9/10): 503–16.

Boston University Center for Psychiatric Rehabilitation. 2013. "Facts Sheets and Scenarios for Employers: Job Accommodations for Employees with Mental Health Conditions." https://cpr.bu.edu/wp-content/uploads/2013/12/Job-Acc-Fact-andScenarios.pdf.

Bress, Andrea. 2013. "Making Your School Library More Functional to Individuals with Autism." *Library Media Connection* 32: 46–47.

Brown, Lydia X. Z. 2012. *Ableist Words and Terms to Avoid.* Autistic Hoya. www.autistichoya.com/p/ableist-words-and-terms-to-avoid.html.

Dierks, Kevin, Rich Kelly, Lily Matsubara, Juliana R. Romero, and Kiriko Takahashi. 2007. "Disability Awareness Toolkit." University of Hawai'i at Mānoa, Center on Disability Studies. www.ist.hawaii.edu/products/toolkits/pdf/DisabilityAwarenessToolkit.pdf.

Grassi, Renee, and Holly Jin. 2015. "Accessible to All: Serving Youth and Young Adults with Disabilities [RAILS Webinar]." December 15. www.youtube.com/watch?v=QEQTFdDGWR4.

Harpur, Paul, and Rebecca Loudoun. 2011. "The Barrier of the Written Word: Analysing Universities' Policies to Students with Print Disabilities." *Journal of Higher Education Policy and Management* 33 (2): 153–67.

Hyder, Eileen, and Cathy Tissot. 2013. "'That's Definite Discrimination': Practice under the Umbrella of Inclusion." *Disability and Society* 28 (1): 1–13.

Lemle, Janet, Hannah Martinez, Suzanne McGowan, and Marsha Marcilla. 2016. "AnyAbility: Taking Ordinary Service for Adults with Disabilities to an Extraordinary Level." Public Library Association Annual Conference, Denver, CO. April 7. www.placonference.org/program/anyability-taking-ordinary-service-for-adults-with-disabilities-to-an-extraordinary-level.

McHone-Chase, Sarah. 2009. "Privacy and Confidentiality Issues: A Guide for Libraries and Their Lawyers." *Reference and User Services Quarterly* 49 (1): 104–5.

McNulty, Tom. 1999. "Introduction." *Accessible Libraries on Campus: A Practical Guide for the Creation of Disability-Friendly Libraries.* Chicago: Association of College and Research Libraries.

National Center on Workforce Disability. 2008. "Watch Your Language." www.onestops.info/article.php?article_id=14.

National Library Service. 2016. "Reference Publications." www.loc.gov/nls/reference/index.html.

Osborne, Robin, and the American Library Association. Office for Literacy and Outreach Services. 2004. *From Outreach to Equity: Innovative Models of Library Policy and Practice.* Chicago: American Library Association.

Rutledge, Lorelei. 2014. "Working with Patrons with Disabilities: How Do I Get Started?" American Library Association. www.ala.org/nmrt/news/footnotes/november2014/working-patrons-disabilities-how-do-i-get-started-lorelei-rutledge-ala-library-services-people.

Thompson-Ebanks, Valerie. 2014. "Voluntary Withdrawal of College Juniors and Seniors with Non-Apparent Disabilities: Family, Peers, and Institutional Factors." *Journal of Sociology* 2 (2): 111–34.

United Spinal Association. 2008. *Disability Etiquette: Tips on Interacting with People with Disabilities.* Jackson Heights, NY. www.unitedspinal.org/pdf/DisabilityEtiquette.pdf.

United States Department of Agriculture. Agriculture Cooperative Service. 1990. *Cooperative Information Report 39: Sample Policies for Cooperatives.* www.rd.usda.gov/files/cir39.pdf.

United States Government and Equal Employment Opportunity Commission. "The Americans with Disabilities Act Title II Technical Assistance Manual." www.ada.gov/taman2.html and https://askjan.org/links/ADAtam1.html.

Wallis, Pete. 2010. *Are You Okay?: A Practical Guide to Helping Young Victims of Crime.* London: Jessica Kingsley Publishers.

Winter, Matt. 2011. *Asperger Syndrome: What Teachers Need to Know.* New York: Jessica Kingsley Publishers.

Young, Richard A., Sheila K. Marshall, Ladislav Valach, Jose Domene, Matthew D. Graham, and Anat Zaidman-Zait. 2010. *Transition to Adulthood: Action, Projects, and Counseling.* New York: Springer Science and Business Media.

# CHAPTER 3

# Setting Up Facilities

THIS CHAPTER WILL DISCUSS DESIGNING, UPGRADING, AND retrofitting library facilities to meet the needs of a variety of users, including those with physical disabilities, with hearing and vision difficulties, and with "invisible" issues like learning disabilities or communication processing disorders. Because guidelines are updated frequently, it is prudent to check the suggestions below against the most recent ADA laws and advice available.

This chapter is based on many up-to-date sources that will help librarians and educators remain current on the legal requirements for providing accessible facilities at their libraries. Moreover, many best practices and sound decisions are demonstrated by libraries both in your local area and around the country. Details and photos are easily found online.

We will describe some of the most common and innovative practices for designing facilities that provide patrons with a barrier-free library experience, whether required by law or just good practice to meet the needs of all users. Many of these recommendations can be implemented inexpensively, and many more can be addressed with a combination of facility upgrades and policy statements.

## Features of Accessible Libraries

The first and most obvious feature to check is the layout of your library. Entrances to the building should be barrier-free, and aisles between stacks, around computer equipment, and in display or browsing areas should be at least 36 inches wide to accommodate wheelchairs. All public spaces in the library must be located along an accessible route of travel.

Because today's wheeled devices may be electric, scooter-type, or custom-built, libraries should plan and arrange physical access—both exterior ingress/egress and the interior of the facility—for the widest possible range of mobility needs. Not every renovation or design request can be accommodated, but brainstorming ways to accommodate the greatest number of people should always be encouraged.

Your city or governing body (school district, college) will probably tackle most of the major building renovations including curb cuts, labeled parking spaces, exterior door push-buttons, lighting, and the like. This is not, however, a reason to ignore review of these items. In fact, periodically equipping a library staff member with an ADA facility checklist is an easy way for everyone to learn more about your facility and its particular challenges. Syracuse University's Project ENABLE, for example, has a variety of checklist items that can be used to evaluate libraries of every type.

Even in older buildings where book collections are located up or down a few stairs, recommendations should be made to upgrade the facility with properly sloped ramps, lifts, or an elevator, or plans should be made to move the stacks or provide paging services. Any obstacle that limits a user's free range of motion and ability to browse at the time and place of her choice is probably in need of improvement.

Also consider whether your facility has any ramps, free-standing signage, planters, artwork, or other items that may be temporarily located in the path of travel. Some libraries put out temporary signage that resembles "arrows on a stand" to point users toward the locations of programs, yet these unanticipated obstacles may cause a user with a cane to stumble. Throw rugs and plush toys in children's areas may also be problematic for the same reason.

## ✓ Checklist

Can you answer these sample library building code questions?

- ☐ Does your entryway or security system entrance area have level, clear, and slip-resistant flooring?
- ☐ Are carpets appropriately secured to the floor?
- ☐ Do all your entrance and interior doors have adequate clearance when open at a 90-degree angle (taking into account space for hinges to move)?
- ☐ Do you see a visual alarm such as flashing light at the same time as an audible alarm during an emergency?
- ☐ Are the alarms all visible within 50 feet from the source of the signal (including from hallways, from rest rooms, etc.)?
- ☐ Is there clear head room of at least 80 inches on the accessible route?
- ☐ Is the accessible route to all public areas clearly marked with appropriately sized and colored signage which includes Braille?
- ☐ Is there at least one service desk designated for lending transactions which has an area at least 36 inches long and no higher than 36 inches?
- ☐ Do wall-mounted objects project less than 4 inches into the travel space, or do they hang 27 inches or higher above the floor so they do not obstruct travel space?
- ☐ Do your reading, computing, and study areas have clear spaces 60 inches in diameter for wheeled vehicles to turn around?
- ☐ Is the height of library tables between 28 and 34 inches above the floor?
- ☐ Is the knee space under the table at least 27 inches high, 30 inches wide, and 19 inches deep?
- ☐ Do chairs come in a variety of heights for easy sitting (i.e., to allow hips to remain at a 90-degree angle, yet still fit under the table)?

## Accessible Furniture and Signage

Once users are inside your building, you may also want to evaluate the ease with which they can experience the interior of your building, and note ways in which the experience of a person with a disability may not be similar to that of a person without a disability.

Consider for example your furniture, specifically the seats and tables arranged in various configurations around your building. Some seats in reading areas may be very low to the ground (like comfy armchairs or couches), which would be difficult to use for a person with a back problem.

Also consider the discomfort that the immovable arms of some of your armchairs would cause for a larger person, or for one who needed a wearable piece of medical equipment to fit into that space. The same is true for end tables near reading chairs, which are useful for everyone and should follow universal design principles.

This is not to say that you cannot have chairs with arms or beautiful low-backed sofas in your library; it simply means that a variety of alternatives should also be in that grouping of furniture so that users are able to expe-

 **For Your Information**

Guidelines from the US Access Board in Section 8 of the 2002 Additional ADAAG Standards Specifically Related to Libraries specify that:

- Design of all public areas of a library shall comply, including reading and study areas, stacks, reference rooms, reserve areas, and special collections facilities.
- Reading and study areas must have at least 5 percent or a minimum of one of each element of fixed seating, tables, and study carrels with appropriate clearances between them.
- At least one lane at each service desk area shall comply, along with traffic control or book security gates or turnstiles.
- Catalog stations and magazine displays must meet requirements for minimum clear aisle space, and adhere to maximum reach guidelines with a physical height of 48 inches preferred, irrespective of approach allowed.
- Stacks must have minimum clear aisle width between stacks and shall comply with the 36 inches rule, with a minimum clear aisle width of 42 inches preferred where possible. Shelf height in stack areas is unrestricted.

Guidelines from the US Department of Justice's Civil Rights Division's 2010 ADA Standards, Sections 225 and 228, recommend that:

- Where provided, at least one of each type of book depository, vending machine, change machine, and fuel dispenser shall comply with all standards, with the exception of drive-up only depositories, such as night receptacles in banks, post offices, video stores, and libraries.
- Self-service shelves must also comply, and include, but are not limited to, library, store, or post office shelving.

rience that space comfortably by choosing their own options for seating. If design guidelines do not permit mixing furniture, then alternatives should be within easy sight lines so that users can determine what types of seating are available.

Barrier-free access applies to tables and service desks as well, which should be of appropriate height and shape. Current practice dictates that circulation, access services, reference, information desks, and the like all have at least some section of the same tabletop or counter that are comfortable for patrons to use when seated. Book drops should be low enough that lifting heavy materials is not a burden on any user.

Guidelines also indicate that seating areas should be useful for people with different disabilities; consider a design that works easily for an elderly person who cannot stand as well as for a teenager in a wheelchair. Temporary disabilities as well as life-changing permanent disabilities are equally important. The types of furniture you provide must be available indefinitely, so that users know what to expect.

Patrons should be able to roll their wheeled devices under the tabletop in order to be close enough to conduct transactions without straining or leaning. This includes making tasks such as negotiating a book checkout, sharing a view of a computer screen at the reference desk, or adjusting settings on the printer or scanner easy to do from a seated position.

 **For Your Information**

Help from a variety of government agencies can assist you with implementation. ADA Technical Assistance Materials from the US Department of Justice, Civil Rights Division are available on these and many more topics.

**Technical Assistance Publications**

Testing Accommodations
Service Animals
Restriping Parking Spaces
Van Accessible Parking
Polling Places
Power-Driven Mobility Devices

**Common Questions Publications**

Readily Achievable Barrier
    Removal
Effective Communication
Tips for Small Businesses
Guide for Small Towns and City
    Governments
Questions about Law Enforcement
Accessible Information Exchange

## Sound, Light, and Comfort

We all have different preferences for our personal environments, and over time these may change or become more specific. The same is true about our tastes in public spaces, and in the ways those spaces make us feel and help us achieve our goals. Sound, lighting, temperature, smell, and many other factors play into our perceptions of comfort and whether or not we like a place for a particular purpose.

In modern environments, many of these aspects of ambience are customizable. Your library should strive to provide as many choices as possible, and arrange these choices in logical ways, so that users can always find the type of space they need for the tasks they hope to accomplish.

Many users come to the library to seek a quiet place to read, study, or research. This may necessitate facility adjustments as simple as window treatments, or as sophisticated as soundproofing wall materials. Different textures of furniture, shelving, wall coverings, window blinds and shades, and even floors deal with sounds differently.

Hard materials like concrete or brick, or smooth materials like glass or metal, may make sound bounce around an area and reflect back into the room, creating echoes. More absorptive materials like draperies, cloth, rugs, and

---

### ✅ Checklist

Do your library signs have . . .

- ☐ Raised characters
- ☐ Braille
- ☐ Non glare background
- ☐ Color contrast
- ☐ Easily readable font size and style
- ☐ Pictograms
- ☐ Written descriptions
- ☐ Appropriately posted heights
- ☐ Secure attachments to wall or ceiling
- ☐ Appropriate lighting
- ☐ Map and text directions detailing accessible routes
- ☐ Any doors, draperies, decorations that may block them inadvertently
- ☐ Audible equivalent options

**For Your Information**

Some accommodations for those with hidden disabilities, from the US Department of Labor's Job Action Network:

- Reduce distractions in the work area.
- Provide space enclosures, sound absorption panels, or a private office.
- Allow for use of white noise or environmental sound machines.
- Allow the user to play soothing music using an earbud and computer or music player.
- Plan for uninterrupted work time.
- Purchase organizers to reduce clutter.
- Increase natural lighting or provide full-spectrum lighting.
- Divide large assignments into smaller tasks and goals.
- Use auditory or written cues as appropriate.
- Restructure jobs to include only essential functions.
- Provide memory aids such as schedulers, organizers, or e-mail applications.

other textiles, as well as fiberglass and foam, can all help to create a warmer space and "capture" some of the sound to quiet a room.

Whether your library windows have shades, blinds, or curtains, it is important to have a way to control the light, and the heat it may generate in summer months, by darkening these areas. Designing easy-to-use window features, as well as providing spaces for reading and computing both with and without natural light, will please many types of users. Upgrading light-switch controls so they can adjust one part of a room at a time, or dim lights in stages, is also a good plan.

Users with disabilities are often acutely aware of their surroundings, especially when those surroundings interfere with their use or enjoyment of the library. Noises from other patrons, motors and breezes from fans, floor vibrations from your HVAC units, and smells from the restroom or photocopier can aggravate all users and may disrupt the work or concentration of users with disabilities in more serious ways.

Universal design principles encourage us to continually improve our surroundings and every aspect of the library as it is experienced through all five senses. Sensitivity to ongoing issues with sounds, lights, smells, and temperatures is important for staff members at all times of day and in all areas of the library.

Those problematic aspects, which are structural in nature, can be reported as maintenance issues and/or monitored over time to determine their possible causes. For example, exterior doors that happen to be open when the public bus is stopped outside might trigger reports of an exhaust smell or gas leak, or cause allergic reactions. Awareness and identification of situations such as these should be encouraged.

Staff members who log these types of environmental problems can learn to uncover patterns that may calm users' fears or enable them to adjust their behaviors in order to avoid these triggers.

Such awareness would particularly help provide accommodations for veterans with disabilities. Resources for further information on their experiences, needs, and partner organizations are easily found online. The West Virginia University Center for Excellence in Disabilities, for example, details many aspects of the veteran disability experience and provides links to many additional services, organizations, and resources.

Those issues that are interpersonal in nature, such as when the strong perfume or body odor of one user bothers another, may result in recommending that either the complainant or the offender utilize another area of the library, depending on the circumstance. The library has a responsibility to treat all users with dignity and respect, and to do this well, staff must not take sides.

## Accessible Staff and Programming Areas

We must not forget the rights of library staff members themselves to personalize their own work environments within reason, and we must strive to provide appropriate accommodations requested by a library staff member with a disability. Some solutions may be as simple as brighter lights at their workstations, magnifying software or tools at a service desk, or a modern ergonomic chair.

Other requests may be more involved, and require office furnishings or floor coverings that do not trigger allergies; specialized computer monitors, software, or peripherals in multiple locations; or modification of the staff-only areas of the building to ensure accessible routes, chair lifts, or an appropriate turning radius in common locations such as mailbox areas and time-clock stations.

In addition to providing accessible staff work areas, break areas, and pathways between public and staff areas of the building, managers may uncover

---

### ✅ Checklist

Ways to improve your staff work areas:

- ☐ Expand and improve common areas for staff in order to accommodate all users.
- ☐ Consider adequate spaces for technology, circulation, and security activities.
- ☐ Provide secure spaces for staff's professional and personal use (break room, lockers).
- ☐ Ensure workspace is appropriate for tasks performed (book and AV materials processing, delivery receiving, materials repair, etc.).
- ☐ Separate office space from the public-service areas.
- ☐ Locate the staff's break room or lunch room away from restroom pathways.
- ☐ Dedicate a delivery area with appropriate ramp access and clear, secure drop-off locations.
- ☐ Consider book-drop security and safety, especially for drive-up access.
- ☐ Create safe and separate storage areas that do not interfere with work areas.

---

other ways to promote universal design principles to help all employees. The city of Columbia Heights, Minnesota, for example, includes universal design suggestions for staff areas as part of its vision, and it has shared online a variety of ways to improve work areas in all types of organizations.

Requests by employees are not guarantees of accommodations, and may neither be entirely required by law nor always fully reasonable. Some negotiation or consultation with an ADA expert or legal counsel, and written evaluation and acknowledgment of the accommodations provided, are likely steps both parties will take, although not necessarily in the initial stages of a request.

Employee requests for accommodations do not have to involve dramatic claims from opponents; in fact, most staff requests can be approximated or granted outright while still meeting standards of reasonableness. When a preference is confused with a right under ADA regulations, additional consultations and written statements may be required from doctors, lawyers, and administrators. Nevertheless, the overarching goal should be that of equity.

Staff members will also need assistance to make programming areas safe and operational, whether a space is used by staff, by library users, or by both simultaneously. These additional programming areas can be stages for story times or puppet shows, lecture halls or common rooms that must be reconfigured with different furniture for different events, or even display cases that may be too high or difficult to open or lock. The Raleigh Arts Commission and the National Endowment for the Humanities have accessibility checklists for other types of areas such as stages, areas for ticket or book sales, storage and temporary units, and more.

Temporary programming areas or seasonal functions are often situations that increase staff members' needs for accommodations. Managing summer-reading program activities, providing speedy workshop sign-ups, participating in collection shifting, processing heavy or awkward oversize materials, composing formal reports, and other activities may reveal staff members' own disabilities in the process. Flexibility by all parties involved will help to find solutions that work for everyone.

## ✅ Checklist

To welcome all audiences and be mindful of individual needs, you'll want to consider the following questions when evaluating the accessibility of your programming areas:

- ☐ Are the parking lots, entrances, signage, restrooms, and meeting spaces accessible for all visitors and presenters?
- ☐ Is the seating arranged to accommodate wheelchairs and interpretation?
- ☐ Is public transportation an option?
- ☐ Will you need to hire sign language and/or oral interpreters? Will you need additional lighting for the interpretation? Will any members of your audience need amplification?
- ☐ Can you share information or transcripts with your interpreting team in advance?
- ☐ If handouts will be distributed, can you offer large-print or Braille versions?
- ☐ Will interpreters have microphones during audience Q&A sessions?
- ☐ Will all participants be able to see each other during group discussions?
- ☐ Are staff and volunteers aware of accessibility features at the venue?

## Accessible Collections and Contents

The library's collections, artifacts, and contents must be accessible as well, with an easy-to-navigate path leading to them. As seen in previous examples, not all items need to be stored within three or four feet of the floor, but clear information about what help is available for reaching, paging, or moving items from the collection to accessible spaces is needed.

Self-service policies for regular or special collections can still remain in place in libraries that serve people with disabilities regularly, but help from a staff member must always be available so that users are able to retrieve items from high shelves, load film onto microform machines, or even turn pages of specialized or rare items.

Most libraries can figure out low-cost, easy ways to meet the special needs of patrons who cannot use those parts of the library facility designed for people without disabilities. For example, post signs in troublesome areas that describe how to ask for more help with an item or direct all users to a service desk for further questions.

Verbal cues from staff members, especially when greeting users with disabilities as they enter each area of the library, can identify who may ask for

 **For Your Information**

The Library of Congress's National Library Service provides recommendations for use of library collections by individuals who are blind or who have a physical disability:

- Any resident of the United States or American citizen living abroad who is unable to read or use regular print materials as a result of temporary or permanent visual or physical limitations may receive items from the National Library Service.
- Local recording groups may request training in audiobook production, and network libraries engage volunteers in a variety of service maintenance projects.
- Books by mail for the homebound can provide free delivery of library materials to individuals who are unable to travel outside of the home due to disability.
- Tactile maps of the building, of subject areas in the collection, and of routes to service points can be made available in advance of a visit, or at information kiosks in visible locations.

assistance in using the physical facility. A smile and nod of acknowledgment can help identify a helper without removing that user's right to navigate and use the facility on her own. Information communicated with discretion and respect is always welcomed.

Some libraries use systems of drawers for archives, newspapers, magazines, and realia related to local or cultural history. These drawers are often heavy, have clasp mechanisms near the handles, or are in tight areas of a room or building, which may necessitate adjustments when a user with a disability cannot experience these items independently and at his own pace.

Ideally, it should not be the user's responsibility to make an appointment for assistive access. Rather, the assistance should be continually available, and staff should be knowledgeable about what procedures would improve ease of use, such as which tables to choose to display items, or which chairs should be moved to create a comfortable working space.

On occasion, the reason a collection may not be comfortable to use in the library environment may not be caused by its inherent features, but stem from the facility itself or the nature of the person's disabilities. In these cases, proxy borrowing, hold and delivery services, and temporary formats may be solutions. The House Report on the Copyright Act of 1976 allows for special instances of fair use to be invoked for these purposes. Librarians should check online for current laws and practices that provide further advice in these situations.

## Brainstorming Future Upgrades

The ADA.gov website lists many areas of your facility that should be reviewed periodically to brainstorm additional improvements. They include Priority 1: Accessible Approach/Entrance; Priority 2: Access to Goods and Services; and Priority 3: Usability of Rest Rooms. All other items are of equal priority once these fundamental areas are in compliance with the law.

Organize a time to survey your whole facility. Decide who will conduct each part of the review and who will double-check the results. Enlist as many constituents as possible to assist in identifying barriers as well as to develop solutions for removing these barriers. Use a blank floor plan so helpers can mark areas that seem to need attention.

Identifying problems that turn out to be within code is not a failure of your evaluation system or process. As other organizations urge us, if you see some-

---

### ⓘ For Your Information

Some principles of architectural access, from *Design for Accessibility: A Cultural Administrator's Handbook* (2003), include:

- Equitable use (provides the same means of use for all users, identical whenever possible, equivalent when not)
- Flexibility in use (accommodates a wide range of individual preferences and abilities)
- Simple and intuitive use (easy to understand, regardless of the user's experience, knowledge, language skills or current concentration level)
- Perceptible information (communicated to the user regardless of ambient conditions or the user's sensory abilities)
- Tolerance for error (minimizes hazards and the adverse consequences of accidental or unintended actions)
- Low physical effort (used efficiently and comfortably and with a minimum of fatigue)
- Appropriate size and space (easy to see, find, approach, manipulate, and use effectively)

---

thing, then say something. Often, it is better to inquire than to assume that things were done correctly in the past. Next, library staff can set priorities for implementing the suggested improvements, or for bringing larger problems that need to be evaluated to the experts.

Can doors be opened with limited exertion in all areas of your library? Is it obvious how someone would ask to have shades pulled down, windows opened, or monitors faced in different directions? Have emergency signs been tested recently, and are they operating properly? All of these and more are questions that your library staff should continually ask.

Universal Design E-World from the Center for Inclusive Design and Environmental Access in Buffalo, New York, provides many more examples of wayfinding and emergency signs, turning space for electric wheelchairs and scooters, seat and table heights, and information on grasping and grip forces for using objects or opening doors.

Are the restrooms up to standard? This includes such details as the height and shape of the door locks and paper products, among many others. Is your library staff knowledgeable about what features your library already has in place, and which others it needs? Sharing this information with workers from other libraries is sure to uncover a bevy of stories about updates and compliance.

Be especially specific when judging positioning of items in your library's layout. Use a tape measure, a yardstick, and/or an engineer's wheel to accurately measure spaces, distances, heights, and widths. Ask volunteers to share their impressions from previous library visits, or solicit volunteers for walk-throughs or "drive-thrus."

Record your measurements on a blank floor plan or map of the building, and note potential problems. Brainstorm possible solutions on the spot and follow up later, even if you cannot implement them immediately. Often, your library may need outside help to achieve the best solutions. And sometimes makeshift solutions do more harm than good, because they may call attention to a problem that does not yet have a solution.

If a solution seems impossible to achieve, to fund, or to work around, remember that this may just be a temporary setback. Keep your analysis handy and note a date on your calendar six months or a year from now to revisit both the problem areas and their proposed solutions to see if new opportunities have arisen, new technologies have been created, or new funds have become available for your improvements.

## Resources

Adaptive Environments Center, Inc., and Barrier Free Environments, Inc. 1995. "ADA Checklist for Existing Facilities." www.ada.gov/racheck.pdf.

American Library Association. Association of Specialized and Cooperative Library Agencies. "ADA and Libraries." www.ala.org/tools/ada-and-libraries.

——. "People with Mobility Impairments: What You Need to Know, Library Accessibility Tip Sheet 4." www.ala.org/ascla/asclaprotools/accessibilitytipsheets/physical-disabilities.

Beck, Susan Gilbert. "Wayfinding in Libraries. 1996." *Library Hi Tech* 14 (1): 27–36.

Brady, Tara, Camille Salas, Ayah Nuriddin, Walter Rodgers, and Mega Subramaniam. "MakeAbility: Creating Accessible Makerspace Events in a Public Library." 2014. *Public Library Quarterly* 33 (4): 330–47.

Bress, Andrea. 2013. Making Your School Library More Functional to Individuals with Autism. *Library Media Connection* 32 (1): 46–47.

Center for Inclusive Design and Environmental Access. 2009. "Universal Design E-World." http://udeworld.com/dissemination/design-resources.html.

Centers for Disease Control and Prevention. "Disability and Health: Accessibility." www.cdc.gov/ncbddd/disabilityandhealth/accessibility.html.

Chittenden, Michele, and Kelly Dermody. 2014. "Removing Barriers to Access: Libraries and the Accessibility for Ontarians with Disabilities Act." *Feliciter* 56 (3): 94–96.

City of Columbia Heights, Minnesota. "Vision for Staff Work Areas." Task Force Vision Statement. www.columbiaheightsmn.gov/DocumentCenter/View/1021.

Howe, Abigail. 2011. "Best Practice in Disability Provision in Higher Education Libraries in England Specializing in Art, Media, and Design." *New Review of Academic Librarianship* 17 (2): 155–84.

Irvall, Birgitta, and Gyda Skat Nielsen. 2005. "Access to Libraries for Persons with Disabilities: Checklist." *IFLA Professional Reports*. International Federation of Library Associations and Institutions.

Library of Congress. National Library Service. "NLS Reference Guide: Books for Individuals Who Are Blind or Have a Physical Disability." https://www.loc .gov/nls/reference/guides/annual.html.

Library of Congress. United States Copyright Office. "General Guide to the Copyright Act of 1976." www.copyright.gov/reports/guide-to-copyright.pdf.

McDonald, Katherine E., Pamela Williamson, Sally Weiss, Meera Adya, and Peter Blanck. 2015. "The March Goes On: Community Access for People with Disabilities." *Journal of Community Psychology* 43 (3): 348–63.

National Endowment for the Arts, National Endowment for the Humanities, National Assembly of State Arts Agencies, The Kennedy Center. 2013. *Design for Accessibility: A Cultural Administrator's Handbook*. www.arts.gov/sites/ default/files/Design-for-Accessibility.pdf.

National Endowment for the Humanities. "Created Equal: A National Film Project by the National Endowment for the Humanities." www.created equal.neh.gov/community/programming-guide/programming/making -programming-accessible-all-audiences.

New England ADA Center. Institute for Human Centered Design. 2014. "ADA Checklist for Existing Facilities." www.ok.gov/odc/documents/2014_ADA _Checklist.pdf.

New Jersey State Library. 2015. *New Directors Manual for Public Libraries in New Jersey*. www.njstatelib.org/wp-content/uploads/2013/01/NJ-Manual-for-New -Directors2015.pdf.

OCLC Research. 2015. "Making Archival and Special Collections More Accessible." Dublin, Ohio: OCLC Research. www.oclc.org/content/dam/research/publications/2015/oclcresearch-making-special-collections-accessible-2015.pdf.

Oud, Joanne. 2011. "Improving Screencast Accessibility for People with Disabilities: Guidelines and Techniques." *Internet Reference Services Quarterly* 16 (3): 129–44.

Princeton University Human Resources. 2014. "Reasonable Accommodation Worksheet." www.princeton.edu/hr/policies/conditions/accommodationworksheet.pdf.

Raleigh Arts Commission. 2015. "2016–2017 Accessibility Checklist." www.raleighnc.gov/content/Arts/Documents/RAC20162017UniversalAccessibilityChecklist.pdf.

Schlipf, Fred. 2014. "Remodeling and Expanding Carnegie-Era Library Buildings." *Library Trends* 62 (3): 556–80.

State of New Jersey. Department of Law and Public Safety Division. "Civil Rights Fact Sheet: Rights of People with Disabilities." www.judiciary.state.nj.us/factsheets/fact_dis.pdf.

State of New Jersey. Office of the Attorney General. 2015. "Civil Rights Fact Sheet: Disability Discrimination—Your Rights." www.nj.gov/oag/dcr/downloads/fact-Disability-Discrimination.pdf.

Syracuse University. Project ENABLE. 2011. "ADA Library Accessibility Checklist." projectenable.syr.edu/data/ADA_Accessibility_Checklist4.pdf.

United States Access Board. "ADA Accessibility Guidelines (ADAAG): Libraries." www.access-board.gov/guidelines-and-standards/buildings-and-sites/about-the-ada-standards.

United States Department of Justice. Civil Rights Division. "Americans with Disabilities Act Technical Assistance Publications." www.ada.gov/ta-pubs-pg2.htm.

———. "Information and Technical Assistance on the Americans with Disabilities Act." www.ada.gov/2010ADAstandards_index.htm.

United States Department of Labor, Office of Disability Employment Policy, Job Action Network. "Shedding Light on Hidden Disabilities." www.osec.doc.gov/ocr/CivilRights/Disability%20Docs/SheddingLightonHiddenDisabilities.pdf.

Vernon, Ryan. 2010. "Inexpensive Accessibility Options for Your Library." *Feliciter* 3 (56): 98–99.

Vogel, Victoria. 2008. "Library Outreach to Teens with Physical Challenges." *Young Adult Library Services* 7 (1): 39.

Wentz, Brian, Paul T. Jaeger, and Jonathan Lazar. 2011. "Retrofitting Accessibility: The Legal Inequality of After-the-fact Online Access for Persons with Disabilities in the United States." *First Monday* 16 (11). http://journals.uic.edu/ojs/index.php/fm/article/view/3666/3077.

West Virginia University Center for Excellence in Disabilities. 2016. "West Virginia Traumatic Brain Injury Services: Veterans' Resource Manual." http://tbi.cedwvu.org/veteransmanual/contents.php.

Wiggins, Jane M. 2010. *Facilities Manager's Desk Reference*. Hoboken, NJ: Wiley-Blackwell.

# CHAPTER 4

# Training Library Staff

W HEN YOU ARE A NEW LIBRARY EMPLOYEE, THERE IS SO much to learn. Not every topic will be given the same importance in any training scenario, nor will you remember everything. Yet even a short conversation with a newly hired staffer to trigger disabilities awareness may go a long way toward ensuring that the topic is not lost in the shuffle.

After training, providing information regularly via staff e-mail or handouts will help any library to formulate a responsive organizational culture. A reiterative process that invites conversation will help veteran staff members "onboard" new staff members with accurate information. Information about serving people with disabilities should naturally become an ongoing part of this training.

Longtime employees can also model an appropriately respectful tone and demeanor when discussing such topics in the workplace so that these activities can also help all employees. Do not forget to train evening, weekend, part-time, and occasional staff as well as volunteers. Training overnight staff is particularly important at colleges and universities.

Bringing together daytime and nighttime staff members—as well as newer and veteran employees—in conversation will not only raise morale, it will help the group develop common goals. Especially in a 24-7 library environment, second- and third-shift staff members need the same special attention given to other staff. Ensure that they are knowledgeable about and comfortable with

**✔ Checklist**

Ways you can close the communication loop among staff members:

☐ Establish procedures for alerting supervisors who may not be present during the current shift.

☐ Report problems simultaneously to multiple managers, administrators, or other personnel, depending on the severity of the problem.

☐ Share suggestions with administrators whom some staff members may not see routinely due to differing schedules.

☐ Set meeting times where staff members can consult with their first and second shift counterparts to share experiences.

☐ Post emergency numbers and official contacts to obtain help with user behavior management from trained, on-site personnel at any hour of the day.

closing the communication loop in sharing both problems and kudos when they occur.

Everyone who works at the library is a representative of its brand. Especially during difficult circumstances, library staff will become the representatives of the values and standards of the institution and the community. They are the ones who are able to demonstrate to the public that their training and experiences results in high-quality customer service and good taste, even in the toughest of situations.

Similarly, trainers must be attentive to the values and attitudes they convey to participants. Unspoken perceptions of bias or stereotype can be communicated even through posture, gestures, or facial expressions, so the group leaders must be highly professional. Choose workshop facilitators carefully, ideally after observing them in action with other groups, rather than just through interviews or word-of-mouth referrals. Be sure to let the trainers know what you expect, and what values you want transmitted; don't assume they know your particular organization or patrons.

Some members of the library staff may be interested in developing training modules for their colleagues. Useful and effective participation should be encouraged from all levels of employees, although their suggestions and materials should probably be screened by the most knowledgeable staff member available. If no staff member feels comfortable taking a leadership role or contributing to the development of the program, counterparts at other libraries or community offices may be called upon to assist.

Just as a workshop leader sets the tone for a day's training, library leadership will set the tone for daily operations and for the character of the organization. Even if library administrators or managers are not leading the training, their presence will signal that everyone needs their skills refreshed and that anyone can be a lifelong learner.

## Key Content for Disability Awareness Training Modules

Information from professional organizations, either in the library field or in other disciplines, can become an excellent starting place to search for content for a staff training module. Free information and quality programs are available online via a simple web search, and these materials are easily customizable with some additional research and citations.

The Association of Specialized and Cooperative Library Agencies (ASCLA) describes a variety of ways to encourage staff to review their current perceptions and beliefs about people with disabilities. Its website also encourages libraries to reflect on the strategies they have been using up to the point of formal training. Many similar professional organizations in the fields of librarianship, education, labor, health, and the like provide free online and printed materials to support these efforts.

Also, consider the resources from the Center for Universal Design in Education (CUDE) in the state of Washington. Its DO-IT Center website provides guidance for creating barrier-free learning environments that are beneficial for both trainers and learners. These materials may also help staff create and fulfill learning objectives for a diverse employee group. Many similar materials are freely available and discoverable via the usual web search engines as well as popular article databases.

The need for common courtesy must be made explicit during training. Listening techniques, conscious word choice, and sensitivity to one's own actions and reactions are important discussion topics. These strategies can be taught either via didactic activities that help participants to list possible steps they could take to reach target inclusiveness behaviors, or via scenarios in which options are discussed and then chosen.

As you can see, there are often multiple correct answers to questions about disabilities. Training activities such as this matching exercise can be modified easily based on the age range of your staff or inspired by current events. For example, news items, legal cases, or ADA regulations themselves can be items to match with their topics or definitions. Other styles of activities can include fill-in-the-blank exercises for groups, scenarios with questions, or true/false items about disabilities topics (which will likely require good decision making in potentially gray areas).

---

Sample training exercise. Match the famous people with their disabilities:

| | |
|---|---|
| 1. Ray Charles | a. Epilepsy |
| 2. Bruce Willis | b. Lou Gehrig's Disease (ALS) |
| 3. Woodrow Wilson | c. Dyslexia |
| 4. Helen Keller | d. Visual Impairment |
| 5. Susan Boyle | e. Stuttering |
| 6. Vincent van Gogh | f. Aphasia |
| 7. Stephen Hawking | g. ADHD |
| 8. Thomas Edison | h. Hearing Impairment |
| 9. Stephen Spielberg | i. Autism Spectrum Disorder |
| 10. Jim Carrey | j. Schizophrenia |

Answers (which will also spark discussion about insaccurate and reliable sources!: 1-d;  2-e;  3-c;  4-d, h;  5-a, i;  6-a;  7-b;  8-c, g, h, i;  9-c;  10-c, g

---

Accessibility features of iPads, MacBook computers, Microsoft Windows workstations, or other technologies can also become content for training. Libraries constantly receive questions about consumer electronics because there always seems to be a service gap among the creators and users of technology hardware. Even sophisticated computer users can benefit from periodic training and reminders, and this can provide train-the-trainer opportunities for both staff and patrons.

Article databases and books can be used as shared readings for staff. Psychology articles about how to deal with difficult behaviors, or communication articles about how to talk without demeaning others unintentionally, are common items to discuss. Similarly, using literature can help to shed light on former tendencies or bad habits of staff in a way that does not point fingers at those who were wrong, but rather focuses on better solutions from the experts in dealing with problems.

## Design Parameters of an
## Inclusive Staff Training Program

Training others about sensitive topics such as disabilities or change is challenging in many ways. Library leaders and presentation speakers must establish effective contexts that will ensure that professional development goes
smoothly for all involved.

Time should be set aside for directed reflection on personal biases and feelings about disabilities. Individual staff members will need to reflect on atti-
tudinal barriers, sometimes with help from a trusted peer or outside expert.
Because daily reactions are often based on long-held attitudes and perceptions, which are continually molded by people's personal experiences in the
world, it will take some time for them to change. Yet awareness of bias in one's
own reactions is an important first step.

The Centers for Accessible Living in Kentucky, for example, use a list of
attitudes to prompt these kinds of reflective analyses. Its materials explain
commonly held yet problematic themes such as inferiority, stereotype, fear,
and denial. Keep in mind that defensive behaviors will naturally occur when
sensitive issues arise in group discussions, so this is not a weakness of your
training program, but may instead be a sign that progress is being made.

Self-awareness exercises that can also be done at home, away from the
group, and either before or after training can extend both the depth and the
reach of your training programs. Encouraging staff members to find and share
informative websites on disabilities topics may also help to involve them in
those aspects they find most interesting or challenging, especially if they have
time to ponder these items in advance.

During group discussions, many errors in choices of language or examples
inevitably will be made if everyone is being honest and open in discussion.
Facilitators should help attendees police themselves by setting ground rules
for conversations and by enabling individuals to speak up to help the group
self-correct when the conversation gets off track.

Some individuals will be embarrassed if facilitators correct perceptions and
behaviors in front of the group, no matter how well-meaning those teachable
moments may be. Leaders should talk with some of the attendees in advance
of the presentation to determine their comfort levels for participating within
the larger group. Trainers may also procure consent in advance from some
participants to receive corrective feedback from the trainers during the ses-

---

### ✅ Checklist

Some ground rules for discussions during training:

- ☐ Speak for yourself, giving your own opinions, not the opinions of others.
- ☐ Honest feelings and experiences are better than advice.
- ☐ Listen first, and curb your urge to judge.
- ☐ Participate actively by focusing your attention on those speaking.
- ☐ Examples shared at work or during training must be kept confidential.

---

sion. These advanced planning activities may provide a useful strategy to deliver difficult messages.

Health and safety issues and procedures must also be explicitly discussed in relation to patrons as well as for library staff themselves. This includes providing information on maintaining physical health and mental health, which also relates to daily behaviors. Consider connecting with other organizations in the community that provide these services and inviting them to present on areas of their expertise.

Tracking attendance is especially important for training sequences. Explain that attendance is mandatory, and provide catch-up sessions similar in style and scope to those originally offered. Attrition is usually a sign of discomfort, so ensuring that all employees are trained in an effective and efficient manner that speaks to their own needs is not only important, but essential to ensure compliance.

Just as marketing materials should accurately reflect what the library does (or doesn't do), employee handbooks should be updated to reflect current training information, procedures, and service standards for staff. Encoding training messages into daily routines, procedures, and policies is an effective way to reinforce the values of the organization and ensure that all employees are informed of and accountable for best practices in this area.

Definitions of "best practices" naturally change over time, so it is important to access updated information each year. When researching possible topics and resources to be used as workshop content, new resources should be identified, and current resources checked for accuracy. Content related to definitions of disability, the ADA, communication, and accommodations are

---

✓ **Checklist**

Library staff can learn increasingly effective strategies related to:

- ☐ Active listening
- ☐ Identifying bias in themselves and others
- ☐ Maintaining dignity while informing or correcting
- ☐ Evaluating possible courses of action
- ☐ Predicting effects of different courses of action
- ☐ Any new or temporary procedures
- ☐ All of the services that the library provides

---

always important topics, but they will probably be described in different ways over time in order to comply with new laws and current characteristics of our modern society.

## Involving People with Disabilities to Assist with Training

People with disabilities will expect staff to have the same expectations of them as they do for other library users. In fact, this practice actually promotes equity among users, and maintains fairness for everyone involved. So it is important that library staff learn to solicit individuals with disabilities for feedback on specific ways to help meet these universal expectations.

On the other hand, library staff members also need to know the range of library users' needs, including those requests that occur most frequently. Staff must also understand the parameters for serving users with more complex needs, including when to step in and help as well as when to say no firmly. Involving people with disabilities to help develop and carry out staff training is a way to ensure that a sufficiently broad overview (as well as attention to the details) will be accomplished.

Some recurring issues may be identified by regular patrons, such as complaints about time spent standing in line or carrying items, or not being able to find an available seat in a reading area or at a computer station. Simple issues can be modified immediately after a focus-group session. More complex solutions can be brought to management or developed in teams. Regular library users can simply be asked for their opinions on what should be covered in staff training if they have time to discuss it while they are visiting the library.

At a round-table meeting, or even a synchronous online group discussion, library users will be able to offer their feedback about using your library through the lens of their own disabilities. They should be encouraged to report situations that prompted them to feel embarrassed or guilty when interacting with others, or to feel disappointed or angry when others patronized them or were insensitive to their needs. Details are often more helpful than generalizations.

At meetings with library users who have disabilities, staff may be able to share additional reactions to their own experiences at the library. Respectful interactions can easily be modeled and corrective feedback shared transparently in meetings where inclusiveness is both the goal and the topic at hand. Time spent interacting with users in this way is always valuable, and usually inspiring for all involved. Sharing information that helps to get everyone's needs met can be a cathartic and fulfilling experience that demonstrates the values of your library.

In addition, providing comment boxes to collect suggestions in person and online can produce valuable information from patrons and staff, even anonymously. Comments should be solicited from users with and without disabilities, because multiple observations from a broad user base will better inform the process. Library patrons who themselves have expertise in a particular area because of their profession or experiences with friends or relatives may also offer useful suggestions for the future in addition to helping report current problems.

In addition to general seasonal inquiries, the library can solicit feedback from users more frequently about smaller projects or ideas. For example, the library may want to provide headphones or USB drives for a small price at the circulation desk or via a vending machine for the convenience of patrons. Offering this as a self-serve option allows users to bypass unnecessary human interactions that may be stressful or too intrusive (or too slow!).

Just like the self-checkout lines in stores, similar options could be explored to meet the needs of library users who neither need nor want direct services from staff members. Both formal and informal polls can be conducted over a two- or three-week period to gather reactions to this idea and to collect details about which matters users find most important. This feedback can be shared with users in aggregate form via a flier on a bulletin board, a social media announcement, or web page news story.

## Video and Online Training Resources

ASCLA's AccessAbility Academy module, entitled "Positive Interactions: Making the Library a Welcoming and Empowering Place for People with Disabilities," is an online webcast tutorial for library employees. As part of a daylong seminar mediated by a leader, or an individual tutorial that can be used online at home, resources such as this can provide information useful for disabilities awareness training for all staff members.

For example, as part of this tutorial, attendees are asked to review scenarios with library patrons and determine the best course of action; correct answers are most likely more detail-oriented and thought-provoking than staff may anticipate, making these modules valuable and educational even for staff who are experienced with these issues.

Tap into resources from your current library vendors to remind yourself of new books or media on accessibility topics or disabilities issues. Some library products or resources to which your institution already subscribes may have accompanying training modules, and videos, handouts, or tips sheets. Be sure to check for materials that may already exist on these subjects before creating your own. If you do create your own materials, share them with others!

You may also ask vendors directly to provide new screencast videos or make ADA-compliant adjustments to their products, should none exist. In exchange for their cooperation and interest, advocate for those vendors who have already added transcripts and captioning to their existing products.

---

 **For Your Information**

A few movies for teaching about autism and other disabilities:

- *Adam* (2009)
- *Arts: A Film about Possibilities, Disabilities and the Arts* (2009)
- *The Curious Case of the Dog in the Night-Time* (2012)
- *The Devil and Daniel Johnston* (2005)
- *Girlfriend* (2011)
- *James Castle: Portrait of an Artist* (2008)
- *King Gimp* (1999)
- *Mozart and the Whale* (2005)
- *Music Within: Anyone Can Change the World* (2007)
- *Temple Grandin* (2010)
- *Warrior Champions: From Baghdad to Beijing* (2010)

When training staff members, sensitivity to learning styles is also important. Video clips from YouTube or short segments of Hollywood movies can demonstrate more complex situations such as how to interact with service animals or how to speak with a user who relies on a handheld communication board or mobile or augmentative voicing device. This allows all staff members to view multiple examples of interactions rather than relying on input from only a few voices to point out flaws.

Because many library interactions will be one-time exchanges between a user and a particular library staff member, and the same staff members may not be always be present, it is important to have online training modules that reflect this idea. Each user will be unique, as will each request, so flexibility in communication styles will be important. Keeping a log of requests could be useful so that staff can pass along information about what is encountered across shifts. However, be sure to adhere to privacy laws in doing so.

Users who want to learn more about the library will also need some services adapted so it can be used effectively. For example, home delivery of training videos in older formats may be necessary for some patrons who only have access to technologies like VHS or DVD players. Likewise, loans of newer formats may need to be accompanied by training in how to use the equipment that will display them, such as cell phones and tablets. Not everyone has access to the Internet at home.

As users and technologies become increasingly sophisticated, so should librarians' efforts. Improvements of online library tutorials, employee training modules, or database use directions should be continually solicited. New information on any of these topics can be found by typing a few keywords into your favorite search engine, so that you can create a steady stream of new and engaging materials that can be shared via reminder links in staff e-mails or through a comprehensive online library guide of disability resources.

## Job Accommodation and Mentorship

Like many other organizations, libraries need to improve their in-house treatment of people with disabilities too, including both library employees with disabilities and volunteers. It is well within the mission of the library to ensure that users have access to job search and job training information, whether they are our current or future employees.

> ✅ **Checklist**
>
> Possible job accommodations for library employees:
>
> ☐ Provide or modify equipment or devices.
> ☐ Offer job restructuring.
> ☐ Create part-time or modified work schedules.
> ☐ Suggest reassignment to a vacant position.
> ☐ Adjust or modify examinations, training materials, or policies.
> ☐ Provide readers and interpreters.
> ☐ Make the workplace readily accessible to and usable by people with disabilities.

In addition to providing appropriate resources for library patrons with invisible disabilities, libraries may find the need to accommodate staff members diagnosed with a disability. In accommodating everyone's needs in appropriate ways, libraries are able to provide inclusive environments that are truly based on values of justice, fairness, and equity.

These efforts are not simply humanitarian; they are mandated by law. Libraries are uniquely poised to be leaders in this area given the profession's emphasis on equity, diversity, and access. Indeed, all library staff members are able to contribute to this outcome, especially with a bit of advance planning and in the spirit of ongoing communication.

Often libraries offer job placement or internships for users entering or returning to the workforce. Some library employees may have started as library volunteers or in a job-shadowing program in your organization or elsewhere. Participating as a partner in job-accommodation networks can be a very fulfilling aspect of library work for everyone involved.

Reasonable accommodation includes any change or adjustment to a job or work environment that permits a qualified applicant or employee with a disability to participate in the job-application process, to perform the essential functions of a position, or to enjoy benefits and privileges of employment equal to those enjoyed by employees without disabilities.

The library is just one of many types of providers of information for people with disabilities. Understanding the library's work as it fits among the work of many other services, including other types of libraries, will also help staff to determine the nature of their contribution to this social justice initiative. Similarly, staff must be able to understand the bigger picture for people with disabilities when they navigate the goods and services of other businesses, stores, and restaurants.

## Learning about Other Services Available to Patrons

The National Library Service (NLS) and the Library of Congress, as well as local and state technology assistance programs, occupational, and housing programs, as well as other types of services may be simultaneously utilized by your library patrons. Your local branch library is only one of many publicly funded services available to all citizens. Therefore, it is important to become familiar with potential areas of overlap and possible areas of synergy between your work and theirs.

At the national level, several groups create and help to evaluate library services, such as the US Government's Institute of Museum and Library Services (IMLS), or the Online Computer Library Center (OCLC), a nonprofit library network that focuses on collections and services. Because many resources can be found via these groups that will be common to many types of libraries, shared workshops may be useful if colleagues in multiple locations need similar information.

At the state level, library services for people with disabilities will be handled through your state's Library for the Blind and Physically Handicapped (LBPH). Services to special populations in your state may also mean checking into options offered by your state library and by larger county libraries in your region. Some regional organizations related to education, such as an Education Resources Information Center (ERIC), may also offer resources and expertise in researching services of this type in your state.

The human resources staff of your library or of your city may be able to provide standard information for workers, recommendations for the hiring process, or tip sheets for managers. All of these items can become exhibits for your training program as you help staff members see the analogies between users and workers with disabilities.

At your local school district, services for students with disabilities will usually be handled by a child-study team, the school psychologist, or the guidance department. These individuals will usually have connections to other professional organizations, universities, and their counterparts in other agencies and in your community. They are often also excellent presenters and teachers.

Resource packets can be based on organization or based on theme, with

**For Your Information**

**Sample Training Resources Focused around a Theme—
Transition to College**

- Virginia Commonwealth University. "Disability Awareness Activity Packet: Activities and Resources for Teaching Students with Disabilities." www.partnership.vcu.edu/centerfordisabilityleadership/Teachers.html.
- Pacer Center, Minnesota, sponsored by the US Department of Education. "Ten Tips That May Help Your Child's Transition to Adulthood: Action Information Sheet." www.pacer.org/parent/php/PHP-c107.pdf.
- Ohio Streetsboro City Schools. "Transition Planning: Post School Outcomes for Students with Disabilities." www.nasponline.org/conventions/handouts2010/unstated/REVISED_Gertscher_%20Transition%20Planning1.ppt.
- Flexer, Robert W., Robert M. Baer, Pamela Luft, and Thomas J. Simmons, eds. *Transition Planning for Secondary Students with Disabilities*, 4th ed., New York: Pearson, 2013.
- Gunther, Joan. "How Can We Help Our Daughter Transition to College?" *Autism Speaks.* www.autismspeaks.org/blog/2013/05/31/how-can-we-help-our-daughter-transition-college.
- Shaw, Stan, Joseph Madaus, and Lyman Dukes III, eds. *Preparing Students with Disabilities for College Success: A Practical Guide to Transition Planning*. Baltimore: Brookes Publishing Company, 2010.
- Clark, Gary M. "Transition Planning Assessment for Secondary-Level Students with Learning Disabilities." *Journal of Learning Disabilities*, 29 (1) (1996), 79–92.
- Rosenthal, Ellen and Rebecca Hansen. "Easing the Transition to College." Autism Research Institute [with video]. www.autism.com/adults_transition.
- Mahanay-Castro, Christy. *Building Transitional Programs for Students with Disabilities: How to Navigate the Course of Their Lives*. Lanham, MD: Rowman and Littlefield Education, 2010.

spotlights or topics changing for each year's semiannual or annual training. Provide selections from various types of sources to speak to the different learning styles of staff members, including books, magazines, journals, websites, PowerPoint slides, and videos.

Thematic angles on the topic, updated each year, will help ensure that new perspectives are provided within recurring training frameworks and time periods. Even experienced service providers will be able to learn something new when information is presented from a fresh vantage point, and while novice learners will simultaneously learn core pieces of information about disabilities services that are central to every theme.

Thus, it is important to have as a key component in your training any information that might help staff members understand (a) the importance of each staff member's own job functions, and (b) the scope of the library's mission as it is realized in your local community. Personalizing your library's service functions, and highlighting their significance for users who experience challenges, will help to demonstrate their value to staff members and patrons alike.

## Evaluating Current Orientation and Training Practices

The competency of staff members and the consistency of their behavior will be an important measure of the quality of services that your library provides to people with disabilities. Therefore, the most important way to evaluate your staff training is by how it translates into appropriate performance on the job.

Deborah Wilcox Johnson (2008) explains that there are three areas of change that can be assessed after professional development training: knowledge, attitude, and behavior. These three areas can indicate the skill of library staff in appropriately addressing, over time, the needs of users with disabilities. Individual and group goals can be addressed in tandem.

Often, simply an increase in awareness about disabilities issues can increase a learner's background knowledge. If knowing is the first step in doing, then the opposite is also true—if you do not know, then you either cannot or will not act upon this knowledge. But finally learning which things are important, or knowing what things might happen, is a key to awareness and understanding of the contexts in which we live and work.

Changes in attitudes are difficult to measure—and may even be more difficult to change. Nevertheless, individual perceptions drive behaviors directly, so a positive change in attitude should naturally invoke positive changes in behaviors. An open, kind, and friendly attitude toward people with disabilities should naturally provoke open, kind, and friendly behaviors.

Behaviors on the job can be observed directly, or assessed by peers, supervisors, or the patrons themselves. When behaviors are not easy to see firsthand, interviews, focus groups, and self-assessments may help. In any event, multiple sources of data about staff behaviors will usually confirm both strong and weak examples of user-staff interactions.

Other training evaluation models include evaluations of learning-into-practice—in other words, rating the quality of staff learning by how well it was applied in a real-life setting. One way to implement this would be to evaluate the staff as a team, either by shift, by day, or by department. Create a mechanism whereby a compliment comes to a staff member and is shared in real time with all of those who had a hand in creating that positive user experience.

This process should also help to minimize feelings that individuals are being formally evaluated or reprimanded. Instead, it would send kudos throughout the organization for a job well done. Individual issues or problems with a staff member's knowledge, attitude, or behavior can be handled privately by supervisors and documented according to existing procedure. Well-organized operations are usually the result of meaningful teamwork, which should be recognized early and often.

## Planning Ongoing Professional Development

An updated list of best practices culled from the literature or from peer organizations will be useful to refresh a training program each year. Yet the basic framework and philosophy of service should remain essentially the same, as long as it has been built on accurate information from reputable sources and is still compatible with the library's mission.

Any changes made to previously well-thought-out procedures should ensure sustainability and easy implementation. Changes may sound great until they confuse people upon implementation. Running new ideas past key coworkers early in the planning process might save time later. In addition, connecting with counterparts at similar libraries may help to streamline the planning process.

Your library likely has many resources in both print and electronic formats that support strategic planning. Look for materials related to values, vision, and mission planning; SWOT (strengths, weaknesses, opportunities, and threats) analysis; goal setting; developing an action plan; and measuring outcomes. Any of these areas can become targeted professional development suggestions when discussing plans for upcoming training.

In addition to asking staff members for ideas for training, it is important to ask your library's users for ideas. A group of critical friends among your frequent users could probably comment easily on potential changes to policies or services, as well as everything from new furniture or equipment to adjustments in staff behaviors.

Checking in with your constituents both formally and informally is a prudent step in ensuring success. Frequent library users, especially those who are popular in the community, may be useful sounding boards for even the smallest of new ideas. Their influence and feedback may include viewpoints you may not have previously identified.

Whether users feel empowered by a seat at the decision-making table or via a casual consultation for feedback during a visit, they will definitely notice that their opinions were solicited in advance of action. And this is exactly the type of involvement that creates library advocates and library champions among our patrons.

Finally, the timing of training or process reviews need not always result in arbitrary improvements. Once many basic accommodations become standard practices, the speed of organizational growth may actually slow down, but this should not be a cause for alarm. A plateau period that is well within the best practices of the profession may be a sign that everyone's needs are being met.

As long as expectations remain high, and staff member performance rises to meet those high expectations, change should not be undertaken simply for change's sake. Remember, maintaining good customer service takes daily effort, no matter how well your organization performed yesterday. Expectations communicated to library staff will be successful when they become part of the daily conversations and operations as well as part of any formal training.

## Resources

Anderson, Mary Alice. 2009. "Get Your Special Education Brain in Gear." *Multimedia and Internet @ Schools* 16 (3): 37–39.

Association of Specialized and Cooperative Library Agencies. 2010. "Library Accessibility—What You Need to Know." www.ala.org/ascla/asclaprotools/accessibilitytipsheets.

———. 2010. "Library Staff with Disabilities: What You Need to Know: Library Accessibility Tip Sheet 13." www.ala.org/ascla/sites/ala.org.ascla/files/content/asclaprotools/accessibilitytipsheets/tipsheets/13-Staff.pdf.

———. AccessAbility Academy module: "Positive Interactions: Making the Library a Welcoming and Empowering Place for People with Disabilities." www.ala.org/ascla/accessibility-academy.

Burgstahler, Sheryl, and Tanis Doe. 2014. "Disability-Related Simulations: If, When, and How to Use Them in Professional Development." *The Review of Disability Studies: An International Journal*, 1 (2). www.rds.hawaii.edu/ojs/index.php/journal/article/download/385/1182.

Centers for Accessible Living, Kentucky. "Disability Etiquette." www.calky.org/ada.htm#Disability_Etiquette.

Charski, Mindy. 2015. "Web Accessibility: Is Your Content Ready for Everyone?" *Econtent* 38 (2): 22–26, 28.

Copeland, Clayton A. 2011. "Library and Information Center Accessibility: The Differently-able Patron's Perspective." *Technical Services Quarterly* 28 (2): 223–41.

Deines-Jones, Courtney. 1999. "Training Professional and Support Staff Members." In *Accessible Libraries on Campus: A Practical Guide for the Creation of Disability-Friendly Libraries,* edited by Tom McNulty, 147–61. Chicago: Association of College and Research Libraries.

Deines-Jones, Courtney, and Connie Van Fleet. 1995. *Preparing Staff to Serve Patrons with Disabilities: A How-to-Do-It Manual for Librarians.* New York: Neal-Schuman Publishers.

Emmons, Mark, Elizabeth B. Keefe, Veronica M. Moore, Rebecca M. Sánchez, Michele M. Mals, and Teresa Y. Neely. 2009. "Teaching Information Literacy Skills to Prepare Teachers Who Can Bridge the Research-to-Practice Gap." *Reference and User Services Quarterly* 49 (2): 140–50.

Forrest, Margaret E. S. 2007. "Disability Awareness Training for Library Staff: Evaluating an Online Module." *Library Review* 56 (8): 707–15.

Guder, Christopher. 2010. "Equality through Access: Embedding Library Services for Patrons with Disabilities." *Public Services Quarterly* 6 (2–3): 315–22. doi:10.1080/15228959.2010.499324.

Hale, Leigh, Jacques van der Meer, Gill Rutherford, Lynne Clay, Jessie Janssen, and Denise Powell. 2013. "Exploring the Integration of Disability Awareness into Tertiary Teaching and Learning Activities." *Journal of Education and Learning* 2 (1): 147–57.

Henczel, Sue, and Kristin O'Brien. 2011. "Developing Good Hearts: The Disability Awareness Training Scheme for Geelong Regional Libraries Staff." *Australasian Public Libraries and Information Services* 24 (2): 67–73.

Henderson, John. 2009. "Tips for Working with Deaf or Hard-of-Hearing Student Employees in the Library." *Journal of Access Services* 6 (1-2): 98–100. doi:10.1080/15367960802286146.

Jarombek, Kathy, and Anne Leon. 2010. "Leadership at Its Best: Library Managers Spearhead Successful Special Needs Programming." *Children and Libraries* 8 (2): 54–57.

Johnson, Deborah Wilcox. 2008. "Evaluating Training." In *Thinking Outside the Borders: Library Leadership in the World Community: A Manual for Professional Development*. Mortenson Center for International Library Programs, University of Illinois Library at Urbana-Champaign, and Illinois State Library. www.library.illinois.edu/mortenson/book/08_wilcox.pdf.

Kinsella, Caroline, and Connor Kinsella. 2006. *Introducing Mental Health: A Practical Guide*. London: Jessica Kingsley.

Kinsinger, Laurie. 2009. "Issues with Older Workers and Employees with Disabilities." *Journal of Access Services* 6 (1-2): 153–57.

Krueger, Karla S., and Greg P. Stefanich. 2011. "The School Librarian as an AGENT of Scientific Inquiry for Students with Disabilities." *Knowledge Quest* 39 (3): 40–47.

Lazar, Jonathan, and Irene Briggs. 2015. "Improving Services for Patrons with Print Disabilities at Public Libraries." *The Library Quarterly: Information, Community, Policy* 85 (2): 172–84.

Maples, Lucy, and Janet L. Applin. 2009. "Stories that Promote Understanding of Children with Special Needs: A Look at Autism Spectrum Disorders, Tourette Syndrome, Down Syndrome, and Attention Deficit/Hyperactivity Disorder." *Community and Junior College Libraries* 15 (4): 176–87. doi:10.1080/02763910903212911.

Mason, Karen. 2010. "Disability Studies: Online Resources for a Growing Discipline." *College and Research Libraries News* 71 (5): 252–60.

Myhill, William N., Renee Franklin Hill, Kristen Link, Ruth V. Small, and Kelly Bunch. 2012. "Developing the Capacity of Teacher-librarians to Meet the Diverse Needs of All Schoolchildren: Project ENABLE." *Journal of Research in Special Educational Needs* 12 (4): 201–16.

*The New York Times*. "Times Topics: Disabilities." www.nytimes.com/topic/subject/disabilities.

Nishii, Lisa, and Susanne Bruyère. 2014. "Research Brief/Inside the Workplace: Case Studies of Factors Influencing Engagement of People with Disabilities." http://digitalcommons.ilr.cornell.edu/cgi/viewcontent.cgi?article=1354&context=edicollect.

O'Neill, Anne-Marie, and Christine Urquhart. 2011. "Accommodating Employees with Disabilities: Perceptions of Irish Academic Library Managers." *New Review of Academic Librarianship* 17 (2): 234–58.

Rogers, Vanessa. 2010. *Working with Young Men: Activities for Exploring Personal, Social and Emotional Issues.* London: Jessica Kingsley Publishers, 2010.

———. 2010. *Working with Young Women: Activities for Exploring Personal, Social and Emotional Issues.* London: Jessica Kingsley Publishers.

Senf, Kimberly, Fiona A. Black, and Debra Mann. 2010. "Education and Training for Serving those with Print Disabilities: Exploring the International Scene." *Feliciter* 56 (3): 102–4.

Small, Ruth V., Kathryn A. Justus, and Jessica L. Regitano. 2014. "ENABLE-ing School Librarians to Empower Students with Disabilities." *Teacher Librarian* 42 (1): 18.

Smith, Fred. 2009. "24-Hour Service at Georgia Southern University: 1989–2007." In *Best Practices in Access Services*, edited by Lori L. Driscoll and W. Bede Mitchell, 69–83. New York: Routledge.

Subramaniam, Mega, Rebecca Oxley, and Christie Kodama. 2013. "School Librarians as Ambassadors of Inclusive Information Access for Students with Disabilities." *School Library Research* 16, 1–34.

Thomas, Deb. 2014. "Disability Awareness Toolkit Developed for Training Library Staff." BCLA Browser: Linking the Library Landscape 6 (4). www.bclabrowser.ca/index.php/browser/article/view/648/816.

Todd, Kate. 2012. "Beyond Assistive Technology: Improving Library Services to People with Disabilities." www.railslibraries.info/ce/archive/99650.

United States Department of Labor, Office of Disability Employment Policy. "Disability.gov" home page. www.disability.gov.

———. "Disability Employment Policy Resources by Topic." www.dol.gov/odep.

United States Equal Employment Opportunity Commission. "The ADA: Your Employment Rights as an Individual with a Disability." www.eeoc.gov/facts/ada18.html.

University of Washington. "DO-IT: Disabilities, Opportunities, Internetworking, and Technology." www.washington.edu/doit.

Vanderbilt University. "Government Information on Disability: Issues and Groups." http://diglib.library.vanderbilt.edu/ginfo-pubpol.pl?searchtext=Disability&Type=LTR&Resource=DB&Website=GOVTINFO.

Wray, Christina C. 2011. "The Journey Starts Here: Finding Special Education Research in Subscription Databases." *Reference Librarian* 52 (3): 231–43.

CHAPTER 5

# Maintaining Daily Operations

OUR INTERACTIONS WITH USERS ARE DEFINING CHARACTER-istics of our organization. Just as in any business, customer service in libraries is often the defining quality that encourages repeat visits even when other options are available.

When we treat library users with kindness, respect, and dignity, we communicate the values of our institution and profession in ways that are meaningful. Therefore, effective communication is an essential component of each and every service at the library, because it will determine whether or not users find your library a welcoming place.

Establishing a barrier-free library environment is an important step in welcoming all members of your community. Once all of the physical aspects of the library space have been modified, and all of policies have been set in place, a consistent message must be sent by staff members on a daily basis in order to ensure that the values of social justice are regularly communicated.

More specifically, this message must be sent and received by everyone effectively. Some employees may not have much experience communicating with people who have disabilities, but training, patience, and corrective feedback will help make everyone more comfortable.

While consistency in human behavior may be the most difficult service to maintain at your library, it may be comforting to know that it is a challenge for every other service organization as well. Providing information, modeling

---

### ✔ Checklist

General tips for communicating with people with disabilities:

☐ When introduced to a person with a disability, it is appropriate to offer to shake hands.

☐ People with limited hand use or who wear an artificial limb can usually shake hands. (Shaking hands with the left hand is an acceptable greeting.)

☐ If you offer assistance, wait until the offer is accepted. Then listen to or ask for instructions.

☐ Treat adults as adults. Address people who have disabilities by their first names only when extending the same familiarity to all others.

☐ Don't be embarrassed if you happen to use common expressions such as "See you later," or "Did you hear about that?" that seem to relate to a person's disability.

☐ Don't be afraid to ask questions when you're unsure of what to do.

---

effective interactions, supervising, and correcting errors are indeed an iterative process that will continually improve the quality of interactions at your service desks.

Sometimes, library staff may also need to help library users learn how to behave toward each other. Empower library staff to encourage good habits in one another. This guarantees that accessibility occurs in tangible and visible ways during the library's daily operations.

The American Library Association explains that a person's right to use a library should not be inhibited because of his disability, which means that library staff must be careful that neither they—nor other users—interfere with, avoid, or unnecessarily mediate typical library experiences.

Additionally, library staff should not make assumptions about the abilities or preferences of users, about their interests or types of inquiries, or about their ability to understand library procedures or resources. Instead, a simple greeting of "hello" or "welcome" can be used by a staff member to call attention to themselves as the person on duty at a particular service point, without any further elaborate discussion. Users will request assistance when they need it.

Some of our habitual perceptions, or even our natural human tendencies, may not be the best courses of action for ensuring equity. Therefore, it is important that users experience the same frameworks of interaction from all library staff at all service points, and even during chance encounters with staff who are away from the reference or circulation desks.

Users should not have to ask for individual staff members by name in order to get their basic needs met, services provided, or questions answered. All staff members must be able to provide the same consistent and accurate procedural interactions to users so that everyone knows what to expect. Ideally, when someone needs help of a certain kind, she would ask for someone in that particular role, such as a reference librarian or a circulation clerk.

When a person with a disability continually requests a certain staff member, it is important to determine why. One obvious reason may be that the user just doesn't know which library staff members perform which roles. This is a common issue in most libraries. Another reason may be that the user has had a particularly good experience with that staff member before, perhaps because he displays understanding of the specific needs of the person with the disability.

However, certain disabilities may lend themselves to habitual behaviors by patrons, such as asking the same reference question every day, or wanting to interact with the same staff member every day for reasons unrelated to a reference need or a library transaction. In these cases, staff should clearly identify the problem with the patron in question, and then provide consistent responses to help to lessen these tensions.

Embellishments or edits of the basic phrases that will be used by library staff during service transactions are of course allowed, and even encouraged. Sometimes, a user's invitation may encourage further discussion, such as

---

### ✅ Checklist

How to reinforce good communication habits among library staff:

- ☐ Regularly model the language of typical and effective conversations.
- ☐ Create desk notes, scripted phrases, or sample situations to remind staff of the appropriate parameters for their reactions.
- ☐ Point out particularly effective interactions to others as they happen.
- ☐ Ask supervisors or peer observers to give immediate feedback to staff on their interactions with users.
- ☐ Use casual conversations and formal reviews to both correct and praise as needed.

when she starts discussing what she did over the weekend, or mentions that she had a birthday recently. Small talk certainly helps to maintain goodwill.

Ideally, library staff would be purely reactive to users' conversational needs without bringing up new topics themselves. Yet as library staff members get to know their patrons well, some desk interactions may sound more and more like a conversation between two old friends.

However, even the chance of encountering these types of conversations may be very stressful for some users with disabilities. Library staff must strive to behave predictably in order to make everyone comfortable. This includes limiting discussions about the content of materials checked out, comments on users' appearance, or questions about their other activities.

Naturally, awareness of all of these issues should appear in the best practices that libraries establish on a daily basis with their nondisabled users as well.

## Dealing with Difficult Behaviors

Routines for opening and closing the library, for borrowing items, for logging into and using computers and their peripherals, and for carrying out other operating procedures are necessary to avoid difficult situations before they arise.

Similarly, having rules and policies on paper (or wall signs) that are not enforced in practice will also cause problems. Experienced users who know the library's rules can easily see that staff members do not apply these rules consistently.

When some users see a difference between what is said officially and what is done in reality, they may exploit this disconnect through arguments, protests, or behaviors that damage the property or the environment of the library. Therefore, a logical, plain-language set of standards that both staff and users are taught and expected to follow on a daily basis will greatly minimize the number of problems encountered.

The Association of Specialized and Cooperative Library Agencies (ASCLA) details key information that staff must possess in order to assist persons with disabilities appropriately. Similarly, the US Department of Labor's Office of Disability Employment Policy offers many suggestions for effective interpersonal communication.

✅ **Checklist**

How to appropriately interact with people with disabilities:

- ☐ If you offer assistance in helping with an interpersonal problem, wait until the offer is acknowledged and accepted. Then listen to or ask for instructions.
- ☐ Treat adults as adults.
- ☐ Speak to individuals directly when you approach them.
- ☐ State clearly who you are, and speak in a normal tone of voice.
- ☐ During group conversations, remember to identify yourself and the person to whom you are speaking.
- ☐ Look directly at the individual, face the light, speak clearly in a normal tone of voice, and keep your hands away from your face. Use short, simple sentences.
- ☐ If you do not understand something the individual says, do not pretend that you do. Ask the individual to repeat what he said and then repeat it back.
- ☐ Be patient. Take as much time as necessary.
- ☐ Concentrate on what the individual is saying.
- ☐ Do not speak for the individual or attempt to finish her sentences.
- ☐ If you are in a public area with many distractions, consider moving to a quiet location.
- ☐ Be prepared to repeat what you say, verbally or in writing.
- ☐ Be patient, flexible, and supportive. Take time to understand the individual and make sure the individual understands you.

Effective communication is not limited to extending a friendly greeting or offering assistance, but is also about paying attention to detail. For example, it is important to ask first before you attempt to help any user; sometimes the person may not want help or is not interested in using the library's resources at that moment. Personal property such as wheelchairs or canes should not be touched by library staff unless the user invites this interaction explicitly.

Similarly, library staff should not speak only to the caretakers who accompany a person with a disability, but rather speak to the person directly. This will avoid the common mistake of talking as if a person with a disability was not actually present, which would be insulting to anyone.

Even when these precautions are in place, encountering difficult behaviors is inevitable. Even when user behavior is not overtly violent, some reactions may be difficult to understand or predict, especially in users who have cognitive disabilities.

For example, the voices of other library users, or noises from library machinery or even from certain web pages, can be startling or agitating to a variety of users. Rocking, humming, shouting, or other physical signs of distress expressed by some users with disabilities may alarm nearby users who are unaccustomed to these specific reactions.

The need to wrangle equipment or the unusual physical movements of users with disabilities may also try the patience of other library users. Staff should be nearby to help to explain issues of equity, privacy, personal space, or even kindness when these issues arise.

Some types of behaviors may disturb other users in ways that library staff members do not notice, and which other people may not report. Additional

 **For Your Information**

As a place of public accommodation, a library that is open to the public must:

- Provide goods and services in an integrated setting, unless separate or different measures are necessary to ensure equal opportunity.
- Eliminate unnecessary eligibility standards or rules that deny individuals with disabilities an equal opportunity to enjoy the goods and services of a place of public accommodation.
- Make reasonable modifications in policies, practices, and procedures that deny equal access to individuals with disabilities, unless a fundamental alteration would result in the quality of the goods and services provided.
- Furnish auxiliary aids when necessary to ensure effective communication unless an undue burden or fundamental alteration would result.
- Remove architectural and structural communication barriers in existing facilities where readily achievable.
- Provide alternative measures when removal of barriers is not readily achievable.
- Provide equivalent transportation services and purchase accessible vehicles in certain circumstances.
- Maintain accessible features of facilities and equipment.
- Design and construct new facilities, and when undertaking alterations, alter existing facilities according to current regulations.

and individual signs of distress in people with disabilities may also not be obvious to the untrained eye; therefore, it is essential that library staff communicate with each other and with nondisabled users about how to react appropriately when situations arise.

Various staff members can walk around the library's public and private spaces frequently in order to gauge in the early stages any environmental factors that may be affecting users negatively. Library staff must be proactive and take responsibility for maintaining a safe and appropriate environment for all users, and their behaviors should be relatively predictable to ensure a stable working atmosphere.

In addition, library staff members must be attuned to each other's behaviors as well. Patrons with complex questions should not occupy an employee's time for his entire service desk shift (e.g., an involved question at the reference desk). Users should not be allowed to ask library staff to do things that they can accomplish themselves, such as making photocopies or interpreting information they find online. Because there is a fine line between helping and enabling, staff should communicate their concerns to each other regularly in order to present consistent messages to users.

Common phrases that our educator colleagues use when correcting difficult behaviors in school settings may also be adapted for library settings. Just as teachers, airline stewards, or police may use direct language to ask someone to stop doing a certain action or to instead focus on an alternate behavior, library staff can use similar parameters to ensure that the language of their requests is understood and followed.

This decision-making process must be articulated to staff so that neither staff nor patrons are able to make judgments based on their personal preferences, but rather so that all employees follow a common set of boundaries and each individual staff member is empowered to make good decisions at a time of need.

## When an Accommodation Request Seems Unreasonable

The American Library Association's Library Services for People with Disabilities Policy takes care to mention that accommodations for people with disabilities "do not fundamentally alter the nature of the goods or services

> ### ✓ Checklist
>
> Many demands could be easily interpreted as falling outside of the scope of the library's services, such as requests to:
>
> ☐ Provide a place to lie down and rest while reading.
> ☐ Enlist a visiting nurse service for medical emergencies.
> ☐ Install sophisticated Braille printing software on library computers.
> ☐ Purchase a Braille embosser for the library.
> ☐ Hire a one-to-one personal aide to help navigate physical and digital resources of the library.
> ☐ Translate items into another language or into simpler English.

offered by the library" (ALA 2001). With this in mind, libraries must consider the essential elements of a resource, service, or program and then determine if its core functions can be delivered equitably when adapted or modified. In other words, when an exact translation, communication, or experience is not possible for various reasons, libraries must be totally sure that any approximation provided to people with disabilities is not a substantially less valuable version.

The potential will always exist for accommodation requests that may seem unreasonable. Especially at a time when libraries fear downsizing, it may be tempting to attempt to serve all needs of all users whenever they ask.

There are many times on a daily basis when a certain type of request is outside of the scope of a library's services, such as recommendations for a local real estate agent, or legal advice for a question, or even information on whether a new business idea might succeed. These types of requests really require an appointment with a nonlibrary professional who can provide the necessary expertise. Some disability accommodations may also need to be redirected in this manner.

While some accommodations may be more convenient for users, they are often not within the scope of the library's jurisdiction, no matter how loosely its mission is interpreted. A large number of requests for accommodations may be indeed reasonable, but may be either inconvenient for the library to implement, or in conflict with some individual staff members' perceptions or beliefs. At these times, library administration must demand that the law be followed.

Staff members should be appointed to investigate possible ways to meet these requests, whether by inquiring among their peers at other institutions

> ✅ **Checklist**
>
> Provide appropriate accommodations when showing a movie in the library:
>
> ☐ Order in advance and have an English closed-captioned subtitled version of the movie on hand.
> ☐ Know how to dim lights in some parts of the room but not in others.
> ☐ Charge wireless headset batteries in advance and then set them up for users who need them.
> ☐ Swap out different styles of chairs or tables according to needs.
> ☐ Offer clean story-time mats, fidget objects, tents, or blankets.
> ☐ Remind users of the paths to toilets and exits.
> ☐ Model ways to ask for assistance once the program is in session.

or by performing library research themselves. After all, it is not the user's fault that a library has not budgeted for these types of contingencies, and it would be well within the user's rights to file a formal complaint or litigate over reasonable accessible options that were not available.

Sometimes the library itself is the unreasonable party in these negotiations. For example, subtitles for movies or videos may help some users, but may not meet the needs of all users, or even may agitate others. In such cases library staff should inform audience members in advance of the activities and methods that are proposed to ensure understanding from those in attendance at each session. In this way, staff may choose from among a toolkit of available personalization options, depending on the needs of users at that time, and attendees can determine whether they want to participate.

Library staff can brainstorm solutions for almost any type of activity, equipment, resource, or service. For most libraries, providing a closed-captioned version for a movie night event would not be an unreasonable request from a person with a disability. Yet handing a print transcript of the movie script to a user to read during the film would indeed be an unreasonable accommodation for the library to provide. With the widespread availability of closed-captioned versions of most movies, it is not an undue hardship to provide some accommodation such as this, regardless of its cost.

Tours of the library and meetings with library staff in advance of a visit can be very helpful; however, they usually do not occur as frequently as necessary. Many accommodation requests will come as a surprise and may seem to involve a lot of work the first time they are discussed. However, there really is no substitute for following the law and employing best practices in serving the needs of library users with disabilities; there is never a downside to improving access and removing barriers.

Anticipating needs by talking to other local organizations and by meeting with disabled users and their caretakers early and often—before they articulate an information need or interest in a library program—will help to manage expectations of all parties and formulate ground rules for working together. Preparing a toolkit of options or strategies that will be ready for deployment at any time is an excellent way for staff to brainstorm possibilities in advance.

## Instruction and Workshops

Library instruction is an important service that enables users to learn what materials are available to them free of charge on various topics. To forget persons with disabilities when offering these learning opportunities is to ignore an entire population of users who may most need your materials and services.

Plan to teach library workshops in a variety of ways so that users know which teaching styles will be used and which they might want to avoid. Some users will always prefer appointments for one-on-one instruction, so be sure to describe the space in which these sessions will take place, and the scope of content that will be covered.

When working with children or adults with cognitive disabilities, it may be important to incorporate a routine sequence of questions to encourage their full participation and to check how well they understand directions, workshop content, or ways to ask for help during the program.

Workshop leaders can help participants take turns interacting with the material in different manners such as reading aloud, listening to a book on tape, or using screen reading software together. This will help organizers quickly determine the most useful strategy for each individual user, and this will be especially helpful to know once the user attends multiple programs.

When teaching a group with mixed ability levels, ensure that questions of all difficulty levels are directed at all participants. Equitable access also extends to opportunities to interact with program leaders. Similarly, ensure that any questions asked receive your full and honest attention.

Similarly, activities that require library staff adjust to users who may not speak verbally, or who may use electronic speech-generating boards or

**For Your Information**

Many of your children, teen, and adult learners may have hidden disabilities such as learning or processing differences. Remember to take into account the spectrum of neurodiversity among all learners, including these recommendations for learners who may have

- Unusual patterns of attention—help them focus
- Trouble picking out important information—emphasize the most relevant points intentionally
- Difficulty attending to multiple or simultaneous cues about what to do next—use a predictable pattern of words, gestures, or pictures for clarity
- Lack language to express abstract concepts or reasoning—talk about the practical uses of information or skills first
- Deficits in the capacity to share attention and emotion with others, or to understand the feelings of others—provide positive reinforcement to encourage behaviors with patience, sharing, and positive feedback
- Difficulty understanding social expectations—use repetition, routines, and clear directions to help reduce their stress or their avoidance of others

eye-tracking equipment to communicate. These interactions are always valuable learning experiences for all involved.

It is equally important for people to feel comfortable using the library and for staff to feel comfortable interacting with users who have disabilities. Lesson handouts or fliers should be titled with details so that staff members are able to accurately describe them, and so that users can determine whether to skip them.

Workshop activities do not always have to utilize the lecture format only. Some workshop activities can be designed so that users can proceed at their own pace while still interacting with the facilitator. Often, multiple staff members can help assist the presenter with a workshop, much in the way that school aides assist lead teachers.

Lessons that teach computer skills will usually attract both (a) people who know something about the topic at hand and want to know more, and (b) people who know absolutely nothing about the topic or about computers in general and want to know more.

Even with a small group, teaching patrons with differing levels of ability in the same session will be challenging for most, if not all, instructors. Consider scheduling an on-call instructor who can support the session leader by circulating around the room to assist users in following directions or staying on task.

A teaching aide can provide additional explanations as the lesson progresses, or can challenge advanced users by redirecting them to additional tasks. However, multiple side conversations in the audience can derail the main presenter from his or her objectives, so it may be helpful to group users by ability level early in the session, as well as to discuss ground rules for asking questions and requesting additional help after the main activities are completed.

One useful way to prepare in advance for users with disabilities is to provide handouts via e-mail or postal mail, so that users and their caregivers are able to rehearse scenarios and prepare for the activities. This will also allow users time to refresh their memories on library topics or to alert you if they need a device or technology.

For example, a well-designed handout that describes how and why to ask a question at the reference desk, or how and why to search a library database, will include clear explanations that all types of users can follow. Just like social stories, instructional handouts that employ universal design principles will probably describe common library behaviors with enough contextual information so that users know what will be expected of them.

An online registration system, or one that offers a reusable profile over time, may also help to alert staff members to the needs of regular attendees, even if they have not yet met the library employees in charge of a particular activity. This could contribute to a seamless sequence of events when preparing for accommodations, thus creating an inclusive library environment immediately because access is already provided.

Similarly, reaching out specifically to potential library users who have disabilities may increase interest in a particular program or a series of programs over time. Getting the word out about offered sessions can occur through social networks, through announcements and news items in communications of other service organizations, and through fliers at frequently visited local stores and offices (with their permission) such as the supermarket or dentist's office.

## Story Time and Crafts

Ideally, story-time activities are equally available for all children regardless of disability. Sometimes, however, adapted story times may serve some users more effectively. Librarians are encouraged to offer all kinds of options to users before deciding on an alternate model. It may even help if multiple options were discussed or negotiated in advance with parents and caregivers.

Sometimes iPads or tablets can also be used during story times, and can be preloaded with various activities to share with users within the library, particularly with those who do not have these devices at home. Not only would this help to reduce the digital divide, but these kinds of devices may be appropriate for all children for different purposes. Introducing technology use alongside more low-tech craft events or story-hour procedures is a good way to get children used to circumstances in which the librarian will accommodate needs with technologies as appropriate.

Story time itself may be a learning activity for many children with disabilities, so librarians must not expect that very young library users understand what it is or what is expected of them. Many well-intentioned adults also do not know how to model inclusive behavior when confronted with differences among children, so the librarian should be prepared to model and explain some of these methods to parents and to help everyone understand why some children may need adaptations for certain activities.

Similarly, some children with disabilities are not comfortable using craft materials like glue, finger paints, or toothpicks. They may be able to participate in an adapted activity on a computer or tablet, safely manipulating similar objects on a virtual canvas. In higher-income communities, help parents preview apps before they purchase them; in poorer areas, introduce families to apps available on library-owned devices. For apps that can be customized with a child's name, investigate methods that protect privacy of users on shared devices.

Drawing software or apps may fulfill needs quickly, but advance planning will ensure that a similar quality or sophistication of online tools is available to match the theme of the current activity. Songs are another method of ensuring accessibility for all. They can accompany reading of a big book, or can occur before or after a traditional story-sharing activity. Songs help focus attention, and are useful tools for helping to control behaviors of all children.

Providing written or verbal descriptions of materials, creating tactile objects or drawings, or modifying for large print are accommodations that are relatively easy to make. A felt board with pictures of abstract activities or processes can assist some learners in understanding what you are describing.

Fidget objects—small handheld toys for a child to play with while listening—are also helpful to calm children, especially if the same fidgets are available during each library visit. Washing these regularly with soap and water or in a washing machine is good hygienic practice.

Individual story-time sessions are important activities that can socialize children for school and for more formal activities like camps and sports. Yet typical story times may not be the most appropriate activity for some children. The library may want to schedule "special needs story times" in order to provide parents a stress-free gathering similar in nature to the usual library activities. Movie theaters have already embraced the opportunity to provide reasonable accommodations with success, and parents report that they don't have to worry that their child's disability may negatively affect others' experiences.

## Teaching Online

Hosting library instruction or workshops online and creating online library tutorials may actually increase the accessibility of these programs for people with disabilities. Explicit teaching, as opposed to serendipitous learning, creates equity and levels the playing field, making information available to all.

One productive planning strategy is to utilize a sign-up process in which people can identify their disabilities in advance. This enables the library to procure a sign-language interpreter or arrange for video captioning ahead of time.

Teaching online is one way to reach users who may not be able to come into the library building, or who may prefer to learn in a place and at a time that is convenient for them. All users can benefit from simple instructions on how to use the library's resources, whether these are handouts online, instruction sessions in person, or streaming videos created or selected by the library staff.

It is important to adhere to universal design for existing and new online tutorials. Try to embed captioning in your screencast tutorials and to provide a full transcript of what is said and shown on a screencast or other video tutorial. Don't expect YouTube or other commercial video-sharing sites to do it for you automatically, because their priority is hosting and serving files, not ensuring that all of their millions of videos are in accessible formats now and in the future.

Captioning is relatively easy using the YouTube video manager and similar tools in other video hosting services. It may seem to take a long time to pause the video every few seconds and type in text, but these small steps not only create a wider audience for your materials, they help you comply with ADA regulations.

Other types of technical issues may arise with online tutorials, especially if they are inherited from previous projects. For example, if a user cannot take an interactive online quiz without JavaScript, which currently presents a problem for screen readers, then the tutorial is not equivalent and access to that content is not equitable for users. Instead, design tutorial elements without JavaScript or Flash elements, and ensure that all tutorial information—including information communicated through images—is text-readable. PDFs and fillable forms should also be designed with accessibility features when they are first created and before uploading for public use. The North American Council for Online Learning's "National Standards for Quality Online Teaching," for example, gives online instructors many recommendations for engaging online-only learners.

As mentioned elsewhere, mobile access to these online tutorials must also be ADA-compliant, and a review of these features and steps to take for file conversions are necessary.

Low-tech adaptations for live streaming of in-person instruction sessions are also a possibility, provided that the instructor and any participants that appear in the video have signed releases to participate. However, preparations must be made in advance to provide users with alternate formats of the teacher's instructions, and common visual signals, signs, or movements to indicate a shift in activities.

Common lesson structures help everyone to follow the lesson, especially if a computer suddenly loses sound or freezes and needs to be restarted. Have a beginning, middle, and end for every lesson, with consistent signals to indicate when the topic shifts.

Remember, online teaching does not always have to occur within a learning management system like Blackboard or via interactive television. Simple online tutorials interactive can often meet the needs of both instructors and learners easily without being very high-tech.

Strong lesson design starts with an objective, follows a procedure to reach that objective, and reviews or assesses understanding after the procedure has been followed and explained. Good lessons on how to use library equipment, engage in library services, or understand library resources can be made in any

> ✔ **Checklist**
>
> Tips for online teaching from the North American Council for Online Learning (2006):
>
> ☐ Create a warm and inviting atmosphere that promotes the development of a sense of community among participants.
> ☐ Facilitate and monitor appropriate interaction among participants.
> ☐ Build and maintain a community of learners by creating a relationship of trust.
> ☐ Support and encourage independence and creativity.
> ☐ Set limits if participation wanes or if the conversation is headed in the wrong direction.
> ☐ Provide structure for participants but allow for flexibility and negotiation.
> ☐ Begin each lesson with a short, student-friendly, summary statement indicating the goal of the lesson and the primary benchmarks that will be covered.
> ☐ Differentiate instruction based on students' learning styles and needs and assist students in assimilating information to gain understanding and knowledge.
> ☐ Provide extended resources and activities to increase achievement levels.
> ☐ Model effective communication skills and maintain records of applicable communications with students.
> ☐ Encourage interaction and cooperation among students when they are in an online session together.
> ☐ Provide prompt and regular feedback.
> ☐ Persist, in a consistent and reasonable manner, until students are successful.
> ☐ Personalize feedback for support, growth, and encouragement.
> ☐ Model, guide. and encourage legal, ethical, safe, and healthy behavior related to technology use.
> ☐ Provide activities, modified as necessary, that are relevant to the needs of all students.
> ☐ Adapt and adjust instruction to create multiple paths to learning objectives.

format and using any available technologies. The best online teaching and learning experiences are those for which the method, length, content, and presentation are aligned to meet the specific objective at hand for the users it is intended to reach.

## Reference and Access Services

Discussions about how to communicate with people who have various disabilities would ideally begin when new employees are hired and continue throughout their employment via regular, periodic conversations, meetings, trainings, and handouts.

It may be helpful to schedule days for library staff to share their recent experiences and successes to help keep staff awareness current. Even if librarian preparation programs cover this material, it is worth repeating for staff at every rank or level. Often, members of the staff have had important experiences and observations, both professional and personal, which can benefit everyone when shared.

In larger libraries, this may mean multi-department meetings of technical and public services groups, or combinations of reference services and access services members who may serve the same constituents in different ways and in different locations.

Quick in-person meetings at which staff members share their stories of helping users and receive feedback on how well they have followed best practices can help build morale and encourage employees at every level to contribute to an inclusive culture. Short e-mails summarizing the main agreed-upon points, signs in staff areas, and reminders at the beginning of each shift are all ways to reinforce positive interactions and help staff internalize effective practices. Routines for daily activities, scripts for common transactions, and suggested language for starting interactions with library users are clear structures that help facilitate communication, manage expectations, and encourage clarity.

Naturally, no one wants the desk staff to sound like robots, and additional types of questions and interactions will arise that really do not lend themselves to any kind of script. Communicating good news in the same manner that would be used to discuss a lost book can make a conversation unnecessarily uncomfortable. However, encouraging library employees to make good

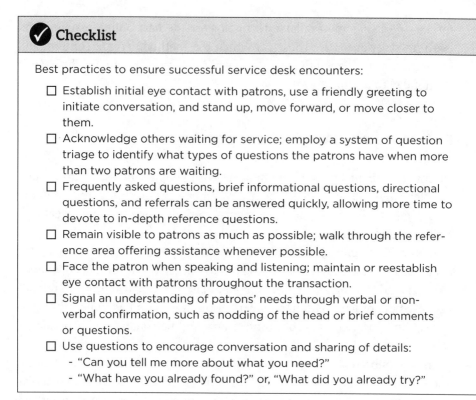

## ✓ Checklist

Best practices to ensure successful service desk encounters:

- ☐ Establish initial eye contact with patrons, use a friendly greeting to initiate conversation, and stand up, move forward, or move closer to them.
- ☐ Acknowledge others waiting for service; employ a system of question triage to identify what types of questions the patrons have when more than two patrons are waiting.
- ☐ Frequently asked questions, brief informational questions, directional questions, and referrals can be answered quickly, allowing more time to devote to in-depth reference questions.
- ☐ Remain visible to patrons as much as possible; walk through the reference area offering assistance whenever possible.
- ☐ Face the patron when speaking and listening; maintain or reestablish eye contact with patrons throughout the transaction.
- ☐ Signal an understanding of patrons' needs through verbal or non-verbal confirmation, such as nodding of the head or brief comments or questions.
- ☐ Use questions to encourage conversation and sharing of details:
  - "Can you tell me more about what you need?"
  - "What have you already found?" or, "What did you already try?"

decisions within a generally accepted set of parameters will ensure that the same tone, content, and enthusiasm are shared with every patron, regardless of disability. Just like in retail outlets, medical offices, and restaurants, consistency in customer service attracts repeat business.

Examples of appropriate ways to conduct exchanges with users over fines, mistakes by library staff, or referrals to a librarian might be written down in a staff manual or simply role-played during a meeting.

The exact wording of conversation starters may differ from library to library and region to region, depending on the personalities of the staff and community. Yet all of these transactions are important, and your examples might cover situations from requesting acknowledgment of overdue books, to how to separate yourself from people just wanting to gossip at a service desk or dominate the time of a staff member, to addressing concerns about a policy or another user.

- "What type of information were you hoping to find (books, articles, etc.)?"
- "Do you need help registering, photocopying, logging on, etc.?"
☐ Maintain objectivity and do not interject value judgments about subject matter or the nature of the question into the transaction.
☐ Gather as much information as possible without compromising user privacy.
☐ Address the patrons before addressing what's on their computer screens.
☐ Be mobile. Get the patrons started on the initial steps of their searches, then move on to other patrons.
☐ Approach patrons and offer assistance with lines such as:
- "Are you finding what you need?"
- "Can I help you with anything?"
- "How is your search going?"
☐ Check back on how patrons are progressing after helping them start a process.
☐ Ask patrons if their questions have been completely answered.
☐ Encourage the patrons to return if they have further questions by making a statement such as, "If you don't find what you are looking for, please come back and we'll try something else."
☐ Make patrons aware of other relevant library services.

Sample scenarios, discussions about the range of effective ways to handle situations, and open ongoing dialogue without a requirement for perfection will empower staff to handle problems to everyone's satisfaction.

Specifically, at the reference desk, users often believe they have executed a library search properly, but the evidence they present to librarians often appears to be the contrary. The same is true for students with disabilities, and perhaps their skill and experience in manipulating screen readers may be additional reason why these seemingly simple tasks are difficult for them to complete. These conversations may seem uncomfortable, especially when users' impatience may be stronger than their need to find accurate or appropriate information. Even seasoned professionals can learn from sharing strategies with each other and talking through examples that went well. Consulting with colleagues at neighboring libraries can be useful, because they may often see the same patrons or may have new approaches to similar problems.

## Showcasing Collections and Services

Displays of physical and digital collections, including unique holdings and online collections, must be similarly accessible as other areas of the library. Library staff must take extra time to ensure that most of your online access portals work with the typical hardware and software devices used by people with disabilities.

It is tempting to assume that certain collections will only be of interest to a small segment of the community, but this does not negate the need for full accessibility and barrier-free engagement with the materials. Especially for digital image collections, textual content must be supplied for each and every image, object, and display case.

Accessibility of special collections can be achieved in many ways, from a printed or online program, through QR codes, or via a mobile app with audio descriptions. Content management systems must also be configured to provide the greatest possible access.

Libraries can appoint staff members to test software settings periodically when new objects in the collection are entered so that ongoing workflows incorporate accessibility checks. And universal design can become part of subsequent brainstorming sessions for future projects, because library staff members can document ideas to be used for forthcoming fully accessible displays. Because both the technically and creatively minded will enjoy working on these types of tasks, diverse teams are sure to produce the most efficient and effective outcomes.

Video advertisements promoting a collection or service must also be universally designed and communicated; this includes everything to do with the content, including choosing examples of the collection that are easily understood by many types of users or choosing actors who are representative of the community to demonstrate a service.

Best practices indicate that libraries must put forth structured effort into all aspects of their special collections and archives, including selection, description, discovery, delivery, promotion, and assessment. This means that nothing should be left to chance or convenience, and that every aspect of a collection's impact must be fully explored and analyzed to help maximize its value in the community.

The American Library Association and the Society of American Archivists also describes that the intellectual accessibility of archival material can be accomplished through the assistance of staff members as needed. Their joint statement describes the responsibilities of a repository in making special collections items accessible to all.

Original materials should be listed, indexed, and described even if they are not fully accessible or cannot ever become so due to restrictions such as physical security, confidentiality, donors' stipulations, and other reasons. It is the responsibility of the library to instruct users how to handle the materials, as well as to provide suitable reproductions to researchers in lieu of the originals.

And as in other parts of the library, special collections or archives policies should be available to all users, with their use applied and enforced equally. Providing accommodations upon request should be the library's default position in policy and practice in every department.

## Maintaining the Atmosphere

Barbara Mates's and William Reed's *Assistive Technologies in the Library* (2011) details many behaviors that library staff should adopt when working with patrons with various disabilities. Specifically, the authors explain that staff members are really at the heart of any disabilities program. Even the best-funded libraries or those with the most innovative technologies still require trained, compassionate staff who can create an inclusive atmosphere.

Special considerations will necessarily arise when assisting people with low vision or blindness, people with mobility impairments, people with hearing impairments or blindness, people with learning disabilities, people with autism spectrum disorders, and people with cognitive differences.

Providing library staff with explicit how-to information in up-to-date resources helps them learn how to troubleshoot problems and encourages them to design positive interactions well before conflicts arise.

The designs of public service functions and technical service functions are important to reduce conflicts between users or with library staff. Clearly marked waiting areas and queue lines at the circulation desk and reference desk, with chairs for people to use while waiting their turns, are essential.

Adjustable desks and computer monitors create a more comfortable area for working together or in privacy. Visually coherent signage throughout the library and daily announcements made clearly and loudly in all parts of the building should become a routine experience for users.

Similarly, wall phones at the appropriate heights, intercoms or emergency buttons that allow any user to call for assistance will help staff deal with difficult customers or situations quickly and with minimal disruptions to others. It should be easy for staff and users to identify how to report an emergency.

The external and adjacent surroundings of the building must be monitored and maintained as well, because they may help to create the first impression of the library's value. Although some library users bring their problems with them when they arrive, skilled staff can provide both compassion and clarity on issues that may be exacerbated by conditions or interactions inside or near the library.

Maintaining a barrier-free environment is everyone's responsibility. Naturally, we all have good and bad days at work that impact our effectiveness and our moods. Yet a strong sense of shared purpose among colleagues that permeates throughout the community mitigates any individual or temporary weaknesses of these types.

Solid policies that are logical and enforceable, along with a careful training program, frees employees from making major mistakes and allows them to learn from smaller ones as part of the growth process.

Meetings that all staff members are able to attend, with accompanying preparation or follow-up materials that all staff members are required to review, will emphasize a consistent message about the value of accessibility as a human right. This ideal will spread throughout the organization and become visible on a daily basis as the library works to fulfill its mission.

## Resources

American Library Association. 2009. "Services to Persons with Disabilities: An Interpretation of the Library Bill of Rights." www.ala.org/advocacy/intfreedom/librarybill/interpretations/servicespeopledisabilities.

American Library Association and the Society of American Archivists. 2009. "ALA/SAA Joint Statement on Access to Research Materials in Archives and Special Collections Libraries." www2.archivists.org/statements/alasaa-joint-statement-on-access-to-research-materials-in-archives-and-special-collection.

Ansell, Gill D. 2011. *Working with Asperger Syndrome in the Classroom: An Insider's Guide*. London: Jessica Kingsley Publishers.

Association of Specialized and Cooperative Library Agencies. 2001. "Library Services for People with Disabilities Policy." www.ala.org/ascla/asclaissues/libraryservices.

Association of Specialized and Cooperative Library Agencies. 2015. "Resources." www.ala.org/ascla/asclaissues/issues.

Bakken, Jeffrey P., Festus E. Obiakor, and Anthony F. Rotatori (Eds.). 2013. *Learning Disabilities: Practice Concerns and Students with LD (Advances in Special Education, Volume 25)*. Bingley, UK: Emerald Insight.

Banks, Carrie Scott, and Sandra Feinberg. 2014. *Including Families of Children with Special Needs: A How-to-Do-it Manual for Librarians*. Chicago: Neal-Schuman.

Centers for Accessible Living, Kentucky. 2015. "ADA and Disability Etiquette." www.calky.org/services/ada.

Colburn, Neil. 2013. "Secrets of Storytime: 10 Tips for Great Sessions from a 40-year Pro." *School Library Journal*, August 8. www.slj.com/2013/08/literacy/secrets-of-storytime-10-tips-for-great-sessions-from-a-40-year-pro.

Dermody, Kelly, and Norda Majekodunmi. 2011. "Online Databases and the Research Experience for University Students with Print Disabilities." *Library Hi Tech* 29 (1): 149–60. doi:10.1108/07378831111116976.

Ennis-Cole, Demetria, and Daniella Smith. 2011. "Assistive Technology and Autism: Expanding the Technology Leadership Role of the School Librarian." *School Libraries Worldwide* 17 (2): 86–98.

Goodson, Judy. 2009. "Narrowing the Gap." *Public Library Journal* 24 (1): 6–8.

Green, Ravonne A. 2009. "Empowering Library Patrons with Learning Disabilities." *Journal of Access Services* 6 (1–2): 59–71.

Hanson-Baldauf, Dana. 2011. "Empowering Young Adults with Intellectual Disabilities through Everyday Life Information." *Knowledge Quest* 39 (3): 8–17.

Hines, Samantha. 2012. "Reference Services for Distant Students with Disabilities." *Internet Reference Services Quarterly* 17 (1): 7–12. doi:10.1080/10875301.2012.652039.

Hoppenfeld, Jared, Trip Wyckoff, Jo Ann J. Henson, Jenna N. Mayotte, and Hal P. Kirkwood Jr. 2013. "Librarians and the Entrepreneurship Bootcamp for Veterans: Helping Disabled Veterans with Business Research." *Journal of Business and Finance Librarianship* 18 (4): 293–308.

Irvall, Birgitta, and Gyda Skat Nielsen. 2005. "Access to Libraries for Persons with Disabilities: Checklist." *IFLA Professional Reports* 89. International Federation of Library Associations and Institutions. www.ifla.org/files/assets/hq/publications/professional-report/89.pdf.

Klipper, Barbara. 2013. "Apps and Autism." *American Libraries* 44 (6): 36–39. americanlibrariesmagazine.org/2013/07/30/apps-and-autism.

Lazar, Jonathan, and Irene Briggs. 2015. "Improving Services for Patrons with Print Disabilities at Public Libraries." *The Library Quarterly* 85 (2): 172–84. doi:10.1086/680155.

Lyttle, Melanie A. 2014. "Technology in Children's Programming: Apps for Children with Special Needs." *Children and Libraries: The Journal of the Association for Library Service to Children* 12 (2): 34–35.

Maryland State Library for the Blind and Physically Handicapped. 2012. "Sensory Storytime: A Way to Make Storytime More Enjoyable for Everyone." www.maplaonline.org/documents/minutes/sensorystorytime.pdf.

Mates, Barbara T., and William R. Reed. 2011. *Assistive Technologies in the Library.* Chicago: American Library Association.

McKnight, Lorna. 2014. "The Case for Mobile Devices as Assistive Learning Technologies: A Literature Review." *International Journal of Mobile Human Computer Interaction* 6 (3): 1–15. doi:10.4018/ijmhci.2014070101.

Moorman, John A. 2006. *Running a Small Library: A How-To-Do-It Manual for Librarians.* New York: Neal-Schuman Publishers.

Mulliken, Adina, and Ann Atkins. 2009. "Academic Library Services for Users with Developmental Disabilities." *Reference Librarian* 50 (3): 276–87.

National Archives of Boston. "Guidelines of the Successful Reference Interview from American Library Association." www.archives.gov/boston/volunteers/reference-interviews.pdf.

North American Council for Online Learning. 2006. "National Standards for Quality Online Teaching." http://files.eric.ed.gov/fulltext/ED509639.pdf.

OCLC Research. 2015. Making Archival and Special Collections More Accessible. Dublin, Ohio: OCLC Research. www.oclc.org/content/dam/research/publications/2015/oclcresearch-making-special-collections-accessible-2015.pdf.

Prasad, Pannaga. 2009. "Reference Services to Senior Groups in the San Antonio Public Library." *Reference Librarian* 50 (1): 99–108.

Remy, Charlie, and Priscilla Seaman. 2014. "Evolving from Disability to Diversity: How to Better Serve High-Functioning Autistic Students." *Reference and User Services Quarterly* 54 (1): 24–28.

Reyes, Ana Nieves Millán. 2010. "Librarian Services: A Perspective of Students with Disabilities and the Library Staff of Six University Libraries in Madrid/Servicios bibliotecarios: La perspectiva de los estudiantes con discapacidad y el personal bibliotecario a través de seis universidades Madrileñas." *Revista Española De Documentación Científica* 33 (1): 106–26.

Riley, Cordelia. 2009. "Training for Library Patrons Who Are Hard of Hearing." *Journal of Access Services* 6 (1–2): 72–97.

Riley-Huff, Debra. 2012. "Web Accessibility and Universal Design: A Primer on Standards and Best Practices for Libraries." *Library Technology Reports* 48 (7): 29–35.

Saar, Michael, and Helena Arthur-Okor. 2013. "Reference Services for the Deaf and Hard of Hearing." *Reference Services Review* 41 (3): 434–52. doi:10.1108/RSR-12-2012-0083.

Schaeffer, Cory. 2014. "Using New Technology to Comply with ADA Assistive Listening Requirements." *Public Library Quarterly* 33 (2): 131–44. doi:10.1080/01616846.2014.910724.

School Library Journal. 2014. "Program Diversity: Do Libraries Serve Kids with Disabilities?" www.slj.com/2014/05/diversity/program-diversity-do-libraries-serve-kids-with-disabilities/.

Southwell, Kristina L., and Jacquelyn Slater. 2012. "Accessibility of Digital Special Collections Using Screen Readers." *Library Hi Tech* 30 (3): 457–71. doi:10.1108/07378831211266609.

United States Department of Justice, Civil Rights Division, Disability Rights Section. "Title III Highlights." www.ada.gov/t3hilght.htm.

United States Department of Labor, Office of Disability Employment Policy. "Communicating with and about People with Disabilities." www.dol.gov/oasam/programs/crc/diversityikplacedisabilityawareness.ppt.

———. "Inclusive Internship Programs: A How-to Guide for Employers." www.dol.gov/odep/pdf/inclusiveinternshipprograms.pdf.

Walker, Suzanne. 2014. "Storytime for Children with Disabilities." www.slideshare.net/isl_pdo/storytime-for-children-with-disabilities.

Ward, Marilyn. 2002. *Voices from the Margins: An Annotated Bibliography of Fiction on Disabilities and Differences for Young People*. Westport, CT: Greenwood Press.

Williams, George H. 2012. "Disability, Universal Design, and the Digital Humanities." In *Debates in Digital Humanities*, edited by Matthew K. Gold, 202–12. Minneapolis, MN: University of Minnesota Press.

Willis, Christine A. 2012. "Library Services for Persons with Disabilities: Twentieth Anniversary Update." *Medical Reference Services Quarterly* 31 (1): 92–104. doi:10.1080/02763869.2012.641855.

Wray, Christina C. 2013. "Practical Strategies for Making Online Library Services and Instruction Accessible to All Patrons." *Journal of Library and Information Services in Distance Learning* 7 (4): 360–71. doi:10.1080/153390X.2013.844219.

# CHAPTER 6

# Collaboration and Outreach

QUITE OFTEN, LIBRARIES ARE ABLE TO SHARE OR MODEL their inclusive programs or their universally-designed services, thus sparking ideas for future services, resources, and collaborations. Libraries present ideal opportunities for partnerships in the community and among institutions with educational missions.

For example, libraries can showcase the accessibility features of their own buildings, host an event to unveil a particular accommodation or service, or build displays to recommend new resources that help us learn more about people with disabilities.

Because libraries offer clear ways of connecting users with nonprofits and disability-focused organizations, they can also serve as hosts for other diversity events open to the community. Libraries can also model best practices and initiate discussions with other organizations on staff training and customer service issues.

Collaboration involves working together with campus or community partners to deliver educational and informational programming for the benefit of the community at large. Outreach, then, would be comprised of the multiple methods used to connect with your new and current users to promote programs or services, as well as to remind them of current opportunities available through the library.

## Community Partners

Communities often collaborate with local nonprofit organizations, support groups, and government agencies. For example, one of our local libraries in Pennsylvania became the weekly meeting place for a new autism parent organization called Autism Cares.

Over the years, the community has been able to witness firsthand how this grass roots organization has grown and prospered. Monthly meetings held in the library community room have been host to a multitude of sensory-friendly and family events including live music and movies.

A few years back, John Woodruff developed a successful partnership with his local library when looking for a location for a weekly support group meeting for persons who have speech impediments. As a person who has stuttered for years, he appreciated that his local library provided a valuable meeting space and resource for the community.

Not only was the study room ideal for members of the support group to come together and practice fluent speech, but it was also a space where members could feel at ease because they knew they were meeting in a discreet and confidential location.

Another example of collaboration can be seen in the partnership between AHEDD, a specialized human resource organization, and local libraries in Pennsylvania, which share a common goal of having libraries serve as workforce information providers. John's team successfully collaborated with many local libraries in the community to host Ticket to Work information sessions for social-security recipients who wanted to return to work. Again, the library was a familiar location in the community, and by hosting such events demonstrated that it was inclusive and welcoming to individuals with disabilities.

Nonprofit organizations are always looking for community partners to host events or to showcase their resources and services. For instance, if a library hosts a craft fair with an organization that provides residential and vocational training services to individuals with developmental disabilities, it can showcase the skills and talents in the crafts created, and also provide information on the organization and services provided to the community.

Many types of disability organizations can become valuable partners of the library, such as Special Olympics, Autism Speaks, and Team in Training, just to name a few. They may cohost kickoff celebrations, information sessions, and recruitment events. Community collaborations can also result in libraries

---

**✓ Checklist**

How to be a good organizational partner:

- ☐ Ask your network of colleagues and patrons about potential partner organizations.
- ☐ Prepare for every meeting by researching the organization and its interests.
- ☐ Be ready to explain the how your library's mission aligns with the other organization's mission.
- ☐ Ask questions to clarify the values of the organization and the roles of different personnel working on its behalf.
- ☐ Share contact information among all project partners and their supervisors.
- ☐ Respectfully decline any working relationship or project that is out of scope.

---

cohosting open mic nights, talent shows, or perhaps a silent auction fundraiser to benefit a nonprofit organization serving individuals with disabilities.

Libraries are not just valuable partners for their physical spaces, either. Programs related to literacy, reading, computing, and information services are also excellent areas for collaboration. Libraries are often the host of authors with new book releases who speak and are available afterwards for a book signing.

Consider the impact a library could have during a Disability Awareness Week by hosting a weekly event inviting new and established authors to speak about disability and inclusion.

In many towns, senior community centers are located in close proximity to the local library. Whether this design is intentional or by coincidence, the proximity to a library is immensely beneficial to senior citizens, who we would agree are frequent visitors of libraries. Perhaps you have even seen assisted living and senior living community buses in library parking lots.

These planned or spontaneous visits remind us to be ready to serve any constituency with information unique to their needs, which can make them lifelong library supporters in the process. Although senior users may frequent the library on a regular basis, this also presents an opportunity to work in collaboration with agencies and organizations as community partners to develop meaningful programming and seasonal events.

Showcases of large-type books, promotion of readers' advisory services, or even recommendations for music and video may be services that attract seniors. Coupon-sharing or puzzle tables and easy-to-find directions on how to use the library's newspapers and magazines, along with periodic refreshers on how to print from a computer and check out items are also usually met with enthusiasm.

Let's not forget that a significant number of seniors visiting and using library resources have physical and/or hidden disabilities. For these individuals, a visit to an inclusive library environment is a welcome outing to a familiar space that can be both intellectually stimulating and comforting at the same time. Displays related to different themes, which include multiple types of library materials, and not just nonfiction books, will attract users with varying learning styles, and may invite reference questions and conversations as well.

Carol Smallwood's *Librarians as Community Partners: An Outreach Handbook* (2010), highlights innovative outreach solutions that libraries can consider when collaborating with community organizations. This comprehensive resource provides ten chapters on informative topics including senior outreach, correctional facility outreach, using local media to reach out to the community, diversity outreach, and community group collaboration.

A quick search of your library holdings for directories and guidebooks, and of the websites of organizations in your area, will provide more ideas for locating potential partners.

Another important source of partnerships is networking with other people. These people include library staff and their families and friends, staff of other local agencies, and the social networks of library users themselves. While it is always a risk to appear too closely aligned with any one group, the library can ensure that it casts the broadest possible net in finding willing partners.

Social media, in-house signage, and conversations with library staff members are easy places to start. Very often, other people know the central "nodes" in any social network—those individuals who are influencers, who can connect two groups' interests easily, or who can advocate persuasively for resources or participation.

As libraries consider potential partners in the community, it is important to be mindful of underserved populations. The Office for Literacy and Outreach Services (OLOS) at ALA provides a comprehensive list of underserved

## ✅ Checklist

Community-related agencies to approach as potential partners:

- ☐ Parent-Teacher Associations (PTAs)
- ☐ YMCAs
- ☐ Chambers of Commerce
- ☐ Food banks
- ☐ Cultural centers
- ☐ Counseling centers
- ☐ Health and human service providers
- ☐ Social service providers
- ☐ Veterans' service groups
- ☐ Housing development authorities
- ☐ Employment service agencies
- ☐ Legal service providers
- ☐ Child development centers
- ☐ Animal shelters
- ☐ Literacy volunteers
- ☐ Police and fire departments
- ☐ Ambulance squads
- ☐ Substance abuse alliances
- ☐ The Special Olympics
- ☐ Parks and recreation staff
- ☐ Museums

groups that may risk remaining under the radar unless affiliated with a formal community organization or support group advocating on their behalf. Therefore, performing outreach to these groups truly creates an inclusive library environment. When members of such underserved groups have positive experiences, it may result in lifelong reconnections with a library.

Library outreach has focused on the traditionally underserved, and the benefits of these activities are easily confirmed via individual stories of patron success, including increased self-esteem and agency; the attainment of self-advocacy skills; new or improved literacy skills; and newly acquired knowledge from time spent in the library environment.

In *Outreach Services in Academic and Special Libraries,* Paul Kelsey and Sigrid Kelsey take a close look at the development and implementation of outreach programs geared towards users from underserved groups as well as those unfamiliar with the library's resources. They explore the benefits of effective programs to reach out to remote users, underserved ethnic groups, and non-English-speaking users. The book compiles case studies and recommends looking at more than one model of outreach, for example, workshops, speakers, and multimedia stations. Additional suggestions are available in other resources, as well, and most are easily applied to any type of library environment.

## Campus Partners

Most, if not every, college campus has an office of Disability Support Services dedicated to ensuring that students with disabilities have equal access as they pursue education. This office can be an invaluable resource for faculty, staff, and student organizations who are looking for specific information on a disability or for collaboration opportunities.

Whether or not your library is located on a college campus, disabilities services offices at community colleges, state universities, or specialized trade schools can become valuable partners for both outreach and collaboration. This means libraries should look at nearby higher education institutions as well as potential partners across the country or around the world who share similar missions to educate and promote equity.

For example, to provide faculty training sessions on autism spectrum disorder, hidden disabilities, or emerging assistive technology during Disability Awareness Week, staff from Rowan University's Disability Services office collaborated with library staff, which included those of the Digital Scholarship and Learning Center, located in Campbell Library.

Various library staff members promote and host open houses annually, offering computer-based tutorial sessions on Closed Captioning and Universal Design Instruction. Librarians involved the Disability Services director for recommendations of assistive technology and software to be purchased and installed on the new computers to the benefit of users with print and visual disabilities.

When Rowan University celebrated the twenty-fifth anniversary of the signing of the ADA in July 2015, the Campbell Library hosted the event with a full complement of faculty, staff, and student speakers, and offered library tours. Naturally, we provided plenty of food and giveaway items at resource tables. The goodwill was shared by all.

This type of event can be held for the anniversary of any special occasion related to disabilities legislation, to anniversaries of important books or organizations, or simply to celebrate. Many educators should be invited to speak, attend, or otherwise participate, including local professors, K–12 teachers, librarians from other libraries, and caregivers of the young and old. Everybody likes a party!

Another valuable partnership can be created with advocacy groups like Autism Speaks. For example, our university partners with the library and various other departments for an event that takes place each April during Autism Awareness Week. The Campbell Library hosts the opening ceremony for *Light Up the Campus Blue for Autism Awareness*, an international program in which our campus participates. At the conclusion of the ceremony, the library tower is illuminated with blue lights, creating a spectacular sight that is visible across campus. Along with other buildings on campus, the library is illuminated each evening for the duration of the event, usually lasting a week or more.

Values can be communicated in many ways to our users. Their perceptions can be influenced as well. Visible signs that communicate respect for others are often discussed long after they have occurred. Those who have realized its value or who have seen its mission in action often enthusiastically share the library's messages.

Undergraduate students are often excited to participate in multiple service projects, advertising campaigns, and social media blasts as a routine part of college life. Providing your most active advocates with a few photos or short press releases will ensure that your message is widely disseminated, especially among those who haven't visited the library in recent months.

Outreach to and partnership with local military groups often develops quickly, especially if your school library has been a central location to display these groups' promotional materials. K–12 staff members will usually know local contacts and can help to make connections among those interested.

---

### ✔ Checklist

Outreach beyond educational partners can include organizations from other industries, such as:

- ☐ Locally owned businesses both large and small
- ☐ Community organizations, nonprofits, and affinity groups
- ☐ Franchises or nearby locations of national chain retail stores, restaurants, and so on
- ☐ Municipal services related to health, community building, or public works
- ☐ Branches of the armed forces, local law enforcement, and security firms
- ☐ Medical offices, businesses, departments, and services

Libraries are also uniquely suited to hosting disability-related programming and events throughout the year. Events such as Disability Mentoring Day and College of Education teacher-training present opportunities for the library to host high-school students with disabilities and provide shadowing and volunteer experiences.

Local businesses may even want to send representatives to discuss how people with disabilities can enter and succeed in the workforce. Such events are examples of campus and community collaborations that are mutually beneficial.

Library staff can also enhance their understanding of individuals with disabilities by participating in ADA committees on campus and volunteering to be a faculty/professional staff mentor of a student with a disability. Volunteer to work with other librarians or boards of other agencies; act as a consultant to local businesses; or share your expertise in blogs, newsletters, or articles in trade magazines or journals.

Librarians are also able to share information among professional groups, whether to just brainstorm or to help each other turn-key whole programs in different locations. Rotating your library's participation and representation in different groups will increase the opportunities for connection.

Another way libraries can make strides toward inclusiveness would be to invite a speaker from the disabilities office to a staff training or public information session on disability topics. For instance, last year during Library Week, Campbell Library invited the Disabilities Resources director to speak to library staff about best practices in supporting library users with disabilities.

Because outreach goes both ways, library staff members must always be open to other groups who would like to partner. For example, at the Campbell Library at Rowan University, staff members created an ADA Twenty-Fifth Anniversary showcase display in the lobby at the invitation of the Disability Resources Office. Web pages, announcements, posters, and signage also signified the library's role in this shared awareness campaign.

In addition, the library collaborated with the American Sign Language Club to host the movie *The Music Within* (2007) at the club's request. This event featured a film based on the life of Richard Pimentel, who played a significant role in a disability-rights movement in the 1980s that led to the legislation known as the Americans with Disabilities Act.

Sometimes creating a spark is all that is required for new ideas to become action. One successful strategy when planning events would be to send an e-mail blast. E-mails are easily forwarded, and links are easily re-Tweeted.

---

### ✔ Checklist

Outreach ideas for Autism Awareness Week:

- ☐ Dedicate library display cases to showcase autism books, movies, and schedule of events.
- ☐ Design faculty and staff trainings to raise awareness and understanding of autism spectrum disorder.
- ☐ Offer web page showcases of news, newsletters, videos, or pathfinders.
- ☐ Partner on public safety and EMS training.
- ☐ Convene a panel of students with autism.
- ☐ Convene a panel of people who have a sibling or child with autism.
- ☐ Select and advertise webinars on autism, or create your own.

---

Even if organizations do not want to partner formally, you may be able to recruit volunteers with disabilities or presenters with knowledge of topics specific to your theme. Multiple ideas can be added to a white board or bulletin board so that efforts can be coordinated or events can be held simultaneously for the greatest impact.

It is important to know about other campus partners who working directly or indirectly with individuals with disabilities. For example, many schools have an ADA compliance officer who ensures that the organization is following ADA guidelines when designing new buildings and attempting to design a more accessible campus.

An executive or manager responsible for equity and diversity issues, or an ADA Compliance Officer, can provide guidance to many departments, including Facilities, Human Resources, Safety, Counseling and Psychological Services, and Disability Resources. Their staff can be valuable sources of information for strategizing, planning, problem-solving, or promotion.

There is usually a central contact person or office in any large organization who can assist employees with disabilities with accommodations in the workplace. As librarians inquire about these resources and find that they may not exist or do not function properly, a simple query may encourage local organizations or businesses to learn more about disability issues. Often a trip to the library to gather information, or to pose a reference question about online sources, will ensue.

Participation and partnership do not always have to be as formal as speaking at a workshop or handing out t-shirts at charity events. Often, true outreach and partnership happen in the boardroom, at an executive meeting, or behind the scenes via politics or networking.

As cochair of our campus ADA Advisory Committee, John Woodruff works closely with our ADA compliance officer to lead a dedicated group of faculty and staff who meet quarterly to discuss disability-related concerns, recommended best practices, and training resources. Many of these early meetings were hosted by the Campbell Library with library staff as valuable members of the ADA Advisory Committee. Participants' viewpoints and suggestions are incredibly valuable, and advisory committee participants are often in positions to empower others formally or informally to act on the concerns raised.

When time, space, personnel, and funding are at a premium, partners may help to fill gaps in each other's programs. Therefore, collaborations provide the perfect opportunity to work together to first secure a location and then partner to promote the event across campus.

An ADA compliance officer's role is to ensure the organization is following ADA guidelines when designing new buildings or working toward increased accessibility. At Rowan University, our Vice President for Equity and Diver-

---

### ✅ Checklist

Local and campus partners to get to know better:

- ☐ Wellness Center
- ☐ Student Health Center
- ☐ Counseling and Psychological Services
- ☐ Health Campus Initiatives
- ☐ Emergency Management Services (EMS)
- ☐ Office of Social Justice, Inclusion and Conflict Resolution
- ☐ Campus Police
- ☐ ADA Compliance Office
- ☐ Facilities and Plant Management
- ☐ Legal Services
- ☐ Special Olympics Teams
- ☐ Fundraising and Development
- ☐ Grants Office
- ☐ Community Outreach Teams
- ☐ Office of Human Resources

sity serves as the ADA compliance officer. These leaders can be a wonderful resource of examples from their experiences.

Collaboration activities also exist outside the library walls and across campus. Recently, our University Libraries Digital Scholarship Center specialist taught a class on accessibility and assistive technology to a computer science learning community. By taking the "show on the road," library staff can promote the value and resources available in the library to users across campus. Through various library newsletters and conference presentations, the staff became authors and were able to share their projects with others, answer questions, and encourage new ideas.

Another way libraries can engage students, faculty, and staff with disabilities is to conduct a climate survey specific to library usage. Feedback on the library's physical and digital accessibility, and perhaps a wish list of recommended assistive technology to purchase in the future, can provide valuable suggestions to enhance the library to refine its inclusive and welcoming environment.

Many colleges and universities will share their strategies for campus collaborations and outreach in the field of disability awareness and inclusiveness if you simply ask. These collaborations can be quite successful in bringing together colleagues from across campus for a presentation on important topics such as disability, accessibility, and inclusiveness.

## Proactive Tactics for Library Outreach

For libraries to stay connected with their users, it is useful to develop a comprehensive outreach strategy that employs multiple approaches. While senior citizens may bring a steady traffic flow into the library, other age groups, such as millennials may pose more of a challenge. In this instance, creative planning and proactive outreach may prove successful.

Today, social media is not only key but essential when implementing an outreach strategy. Library users of all ages are now connected to social media in new ways that provide up-to-the-minute information on news and events in the community. There are also opportunities for library aficionados to check in with their library online, share news or photos, or arrange for meetups.

Some local libraries even have coffee and juice bars, which can make the visit for the user that much more enjoyable. In an age where libraries and commercial books stores are competing for people to visit, browse, and linger, it is necessary to cater as much as possible to the tastes and interests that will maximize how frequently they visit and how long they stay at a location.

Another way libraries can be proactive would be to create a newsletter available both online and in print. Many libraries already produce monthly or quarterly calendars of events. Often these items can be found at the circulation desk, on community bulletin boards and resource tables, and in the foyer or lobby of the library.

Bookmarks are a subtle form of library outreach. Creatively designed bookmarks can provide information about hours of operations and valuable library website links. Library bookmarks can also promote a new resource or service available to users and the community.

Bookmobiles (or mobile services) are an excellent way to reach a diverse clientele of library users with disabilities. Library vehicles can appear at community events such as grand openings and groundbreaking ceremonies, at system-wide or branch library events, at parades, on health screening days, or other gatherings.

Low-income neighborhood centers, childcare facilities, town recreational facilities, retirement communities, and nursing homes may all be potential partners, thus providing easier access to library services in those areas for people with disabilities. Local businesses may also be interested in participating in awareness and advocacy events. Local supermarkets might want to partner on a project related to library cookbooks or books on nutrition. Nearby pet stores may want to sponsor a joint program on pet therapy or on how to choose and care for a new pet.

Developing public service announcements to go into partner newsletters is another strategy to increase awareness of library services among people with disabilities, and to advocate for people with disabilities among the general public.

## Website Resources for Library Outreach

Libraries experience a continuous stream of foot traffic. Your library may already have implemented a system to track the volume of users on a weekly, monthly, or yearly basis. Often times, these counts do not truly reflect library

> ### ✅ Checklist
>
> Interpersonal and media out-reach channels:
>
> - ☐ Open houses
> - ☐ Resource fairs
> - ☐ Talk shows on local radio
> - ☐ Videos on public access television
> - ☐ Exhibits
> - ☐ Contests
> - ☐ Newsletters
> - ☐ Billboards and posters
> - ☐ Letters to newspaper editors
> - ☐ Library anniversary celebrations

usage unless they also include the frequency of visits or "hits" on a library website. Monitoring this information may prove to be a useful indicator of the need to update the website for universal design, especially if a user is searching your website for an extended period of time without success.

An increasing number of libraries have some type of "Ask a Librarian" feature on the home page of their websites. This convenient feature can save users valuable time when accessing requested information, yet it also provides a convenient option for users with certain disabilities to engage in reference transactions with librarians. A user's feeling of satisfaction in having had a successful virtual library experience will likely lead to future visits to your website.

As previously mentioned, some users of a library website and other online resources may rarely set foot into the actual library. Factors leading to users only searching via a library website may or may not be related to their disabilities. For instance, a person with a physical disability that limits his ability to leave his house, or an individual with social anxiety that prevents her from venturing out into public, may have no other way to experience your resources or services.

One example of a library page designed specifically with users in mind is the "Kids in Motion" page of the Westlake Porter Public Library in Ohio. This library page contains links to information for caregivers of people with autism, Asperger syndrome, and other special needs/sensory challenges. The website has two excellent resources for users with sensory and social challenges. Both are downloadable PDFs—one explains what goes on at the library's Social Storytime and the other helps to prepare people with autism spectrum disorder for their visits to the library.

For other users, searching the library website for online resources rather than visiting the library is a matter of convenience—and saves time when there is a need to access information as soon as possible. Providing a visually appealing online presence for deeper exploration of a library website will engage users who may not ever have the opportunity to visit the library in person. Ensure that appealing website visuals do not interfere with accessibility.

Alexis Alfasso's article "Information Literacy Instruction for Community Members: An Academic Partnership with a Community Nonprofit Organization," published in the *Journal of Consumer Health on the Internet* (2011), provides caregivers of persons with disabilities access to newly published information on the web. Alfasso also cautions that caregivers may not be "born digital," and therefore often lack the skills to search the web for helpful and accurate information. Resources such as these can provide much needed insight toward developing and improving library services and policies.

Whether your library is beginning new collaborations, reinvigorating existing partnerships, embarking on new outreach practices, or still in the brainstorming stage, you have already made a commitment to ensuring that the library is not a "best-kept secret." Intentional collaborations and strategic plans for outreach will help your library accomplish its goals, as well as help others—both individuals and organizations—to also reach their own goals.

## Resources

Abdullah, Noraini, Mohd Hanafi Mohd Yasin, and Nur Aishah Abdullah. 2015. "Implementation of the Inter-Agency Collaboration in Vocational Education of Students with Learning Disabilities towards Preparation of Career Experience." *Asian Social Science* 11 (18): 183–92.

Alfasso, Alexis. 2011. "Information Literacy Instruction for Community Members: An Academic Partnership with a Community Nonprofit Organization." *Journal of Consumer Health on the Internet* 15 (1): 69–74.

American Library Association. 2008. "Handbook for Mobile Services Staff." www.ala.org/offices/sites/ala.org.offices/files/content/olos/bookmobiles/Mobile_Services_Handbook.pdf.

Blanchard, Bob. 2010. "Collaboration Creates a Successful Regional Low-Vision Fair." In *Librarians as Community Partners: An Outreach Handbook*, edited by Carol Smallwood, 97–99. Chicago: American Library Association.

Bobier, Faline, and Lindsay Tyler. 2012. "Partners in Accessible Library Service." *Feliciter* 58 (6): 22–23.

Bonnici, Laurie J., Stephanie L. Maatta, Jackie Brodsky, and Jennifer Elaine Steele. 2015. "Second National Accessibility Survey: Librarians, Patrons, and Disabilities." *New Library World* 116 (9/10): 503–16.

Clark, Sheila, and Erica MacCreaigh. 2006. *Library Services to the Incarcerated: Applying the Public Library Model in Correctional Facility Libraries.* Westport, CT: Libraries Unlimited.

Dudley, Michael. 2013. *Public Libraries and Resilient Cities.* Chicago: American Library Association.

Essinger, Catherine, and Irene Ke. 2013. "Outreach: What Works?" *Collaborative Librarianship* 5 (1): 52–58.

Farmer, Lesley S. J. 2009. "School Library Media Specialist Collaboration with Special Education Personnel in Support of Student Learning." *Evidence Based Library and Information Practice* 4 (2): 37–55.

Guder, Christopher. 2010. "Equality through Access: Embedding Library Services for Patrons with Disabilities." *Public Services Quarterly* 6 (2–3): 315–22.

Kelsey, Paul, and Sigrid Kelsey, eds. 2003. *Outreach Services in Academic and Special Libraries.* New York: Routledge.

Meyers-Martin, Coleen, and Lynn D. Lampert. 2013. "Mind the Gap: Academic Library Outreach and EOP." *Reference Services Review* 41 (2): 219–32.

Osborne, Robin, and American Library Association. Office for Literacy and Outreach Services. 2004. *From Outreach to Equity: Innovative Models of Library Policy and Practice.* Chicago: American Library Association.

Pateman, John, and Ken Williment. 2013. *Developing Community-Led Public Libraries: Evidence from the UK and Canada.* Burlington, VT: Ashgate Publishing Company.

Samson, Sue. 2011. "Best Practices for Serving Students with Disabilities." *Reference Services Review* 39 (2): 260–77.

Smallwood, Carol. 2010. *Librarians as Community Partners: An Outreach Handbook.* Chicago: American Library Association.

Smith, Ruth M., and Judith Robinson Mercer. 2015. "Establishing and Maintaining a Library Outreach Program." *Journal of Hospital Librarianship* 15 (1): 77–86.

Tan, Maria C., and Denis Lacroix. 2014. "Disabilities and Library Accessibility: Partnering for Success." *The Journal of the Canadian Health Libraries Association/ Journal De l'Association Des Bibliothèques De La Santé Du Canada* 35 (2): 101–21.

United Nations Division for Social Policy and Development. "Disability." https://www.un.org/development/desa/disabilities.

Westlake Porter Public Library, Ohio. "Kids in Motion." www.westlakelibrary.org/
?q=node/3403.

Willett, Peter, and Rebecca Broadley. "Effective Public Library Outreach to Home-
less People." *Library Review*, 60 (8): 658-70.

Williams, Elaine. 2010. "A Friend in Need: Partnering with an Employment Center."
In *Librarians as Community Partners: An Outreach Handbook*, edited by Carol
Smallwood, 167-70. Chicago: American Library Association.

Williams, Tracey R. 2010. *Providing Outreach to Families of Youth with Disabilities
from Culturally and Linguistically Diverse Backgrounds by Working with Cultural
Groups and Community Organizations*. Doctoral Dissertation, University of
Kansas, 2010.

# CHAPTER 7

# Programming and Workshop Ideas

WHETHER YOUR LIBRARY IS THE HEART OF YOUR SCHOOL or the heart of your community, boundless opportunities exist to engage as an educational partner in the delivery of meaningful programming on topics involving disability, diversity, and inclusion. In promoting an inclusive library environment, what better way to demonstrate and model appropriate values than by hosting events, programs, and activities that promote disability awareness among staff and patrons in the community?

## Theme Exploration

Throughout the school year, libraries can promote events that celebrate inclusiveness. When choosing a themed month, be sure to collaborate with campus and local partners to offer engaging and informative programming. While it may not be realistic to schedule activities on a daily basis, the use of library displays cases in the library lobby, signage near the reference desk, or bulletin boards located at partner facilities can be very effective ways to showcase library materials like movies, books, and infographics related to your theme for the month.

Two themed months that have become staples in the authors' own collaborations include Disability Awareness Month (each October) and Autism

---

### ✅ Checklist

Connect these themes with disabilities awareness at any time of year:

- ☐ Friendship
- ☐ Careers
- ☐ Famous Authors, Astronauts, Architects, Artists, Athletes, etc.
- ☐ Local Heroes
- ☐ Kindness
- ☐ Financial Topics
- ☐ Social Media Safety
- ☐ Social Media Etiquette
- ☐ Technology
- ☐ Health and Exercise

---

Awareness Month (every April). During these theme months, library programming and events sponsored by many other departments take place in a number of campus locations including the library. For example, the opening ceremony of Lighting Up the Campus Blue for Autism Awareness has offered a gathering at our university in which the library's tower was illuminated with blue light bulbs for the duration of the week.

Last October, over the course of Disability Awareness Week, the library partnered with our local American Sign Language Club to host a movie about the trailblazers whose efforts led to legislation that came to be known as the Americans with Disabilities Act. Last April, our staff traveled to partner agencies to attend their Autism Awareness events as representatives of the library, to spread awareness about our own events and resources, and to connect with potential collaborators as well as potential library users.

It is also important to remember that people with disabilities may simultaneously be members of other protected or underrepresented groups. The Campbell Library has also hosted Safe Zone trainings for the campus community. Safe Zone is a training module that assists attendees in gaining a deeper understanding of LGBTQ terminology to provide better support to students on campus. Safe Zone stickers are given to attendees completing the training to place on an office door or in other visible locations.

As a result, LGBTQ students know that a safe location exists where they will find supports and resources when needed. And similarly, students and staff learn that the library does not focus solely on impediments but also celebrates all people. As the library becomes known for tolerance, diversity, and support for all, it also builds momentum and scope for its advocacy efforts.

Connecting opportunities, events, and people may seem like a natural task for libraries. While "LGBTQ and disability" or "military and disability" issues may seem likely combinations of themes, recall the importance of the individuality of many groups, and recognize that the brand and identity of their organizations is important as well.

Library staff should be careful to select themes that are appropriate to their community, and ideally combine celebrations only after consulting these groups. Too many topics, or themes, that arise too frequently, may diminish the importance of any one event.

---

 **For Your Information**

Consider participating in these American Library Association-sponsored events:

- ALA Youth Media Awards—January
- Digital Learning Day—February
- Teen Tech Week—March
- Freedom of Information Day—March
- School Library Month—April
- D.E.A.R—Drop Everything and Read—April
- National Library Week—April
- National Library Workers Day—April
- National Bookmobile Day—April
- Money Smart Week®—April
- Preservation Week—April
- Children's Day/Book Day—May
- Choose Privacy Week—May
- National Library Legislative Day—May
- June is GLBT Book Month—June
- Library Card Sign-up Month—September
- Banned Books Week—September
- Banned Websites Awareness Day—September
- Teen Read Week—October
- National Friends of Libraries Week—October
- International Games Day—November
- Picture Book Month—November

Nevertheless, community libraries must carefully select and justify the list of themed events related to disabilities or other topics regularly. Libraries can explore themed months to raise awareness about specific disabilities such as mental illness, Alzheimer's, cancer, PTSD, or ADHD, among others. Themed events sponsored by large national organizations are frequent awareness topics, but there are many more. Ensure that those you have chosen match the interests of your community, and do not duplicate existing efforts unless it is your goal to explicitly do so.

In addition to outreach to potential partners in the community, it will be important to ask for input from your library staff when planning themes. During a staff meeting or office retreat, we recommend that you assess whether you have resources within your library to provide authentic voices or operational assistance. Perhaps you may have coworkers who are quite knowledgeable about a certain disability as a result of their personal experiences. Any such coworkers within the library would be excellent choices to take the lead in planning a themed month, but it is important to ask if they are willing to participate or if it might make them uncomfortable to be in the spotlight. One may even volunteer to take the lead on the project. Either way, this individual may be an invaluable resource for input and feedback as well as for recommendations for speakers, films, and programming ideas.

While it is ideal to explore monthly themes promoting disability awareness and inclusiveness, it may not be realistic from a programming standpoint. Therefore, when planning for a themed week or month it isn't necessary to focus all activities and programming around disability and inclusiveness. Instead, you can imbed diverse activities into another theme, such as National Poetry Month.

For each of the chosen themed weeks or months you could dedicate a day or more with activities to highlight or showcase diversity within the theme to ensure inclusiveness. For instance, during ALA Youth Media Awards in January you could devote a day to movies about youth who have disabilities. In addition, websites, contests, or news about alumni from your local area could be shared and recognized.

For an existing library celebration or promotion week, you can choose to honor or recognize an individual or group for going above and beyond in raising disability awareness in their community. You may see connections with some of the technology, financial, teen, or other specialists in your town, and

**For Your Information**

Related organizations' events and celebrations:

- Children's Book Week, sponsored by the Children's Book Council
- International Literacy Day, sponsored by the United Nations Educational, Scientific and Cultural Organization (UNESCO)
- National Poetry Month, sponsored by Academy of American Poets
- National Young Readers Week of the BOOK IT!-Pizza Hut national reading incentive program (formerly National Young Readers Day)
- Read Across America, a one-day special event sponsored by the National Education Association
- Bill of Rights Day, sponsored by the US Government
- Deaf Awareness Week, sponsored by World Federation of the Deaf (WFD) and the National Association of the Deaf (NAD)
- SafeZone Projects, Activities and Training
- Many famous authors' birthdays or book release anniversaries

list their accomplishments in a news release to be distributed to libraries across the country.

When reviewing potential items for special book months, you may want to choose a few selections that incorporate disability, diversity, and inclusiveness. Again, disability awareness does not have to be overtly promoted as a special day, month, or week if inclusiveness is appropriately promoted on a regular basis.

Through striving to keep diversity in the forefront of your planning process, you will increase the likelihood of truly inclusive behaviors, with themed weeks or months serving as reminders or reinforcements. This will also provide an opportunity to expand your library outreach efforts to community organizations and to identify new collaborations for the future.

Librarians are particularly adept at seeing connections between topics, and can easily find resources that encourage participation and examples from people who have disabilities and people who do not. Remember to do actual searches in your catalog, in library databases, and on the web for sample materials and topics for bulletin boards, in addition to brainstorming just off the top of your head. A richness and complexity of examples will thus influence your presentation of any topic.

**For Your Information**

The many ways we communicate:

- Visual, auditory, kinesthetic channels
- Painting, drawing, sculpting
- Video, audio, visualizations
- Bulletin board, posters, computer kiosks
- Spoken word, singing, pantomime
- Movement, dance, performance art
- Lights, colors, shapes
- Simple, moderate, complex messages
- Quick, standard, thorough communications
- Individual, partner, team interactions

## Developing an Operational Calendar

Advanced planning is essential as you go about setting a programming schedule for the upcoming year. The authors have found an operational calendar to be a necessity in the planning process. Aligning your operational calendar with your school district's academic calendar may increase the potential for creative programming that is both timely and relevant, as well as uncover opportunities for partnerships.

For example, our university's Office of Academic Success and Disability Resources offers a College Compass Transition Program to new incoming freshman and transfer students with disabilities. During the week of programming, we partner with the Campbell Library as staff members conduct tours of the building while highlighting specific resources such as JAWS and Kurzweil readers for users with visual and print disabilities.

One of the immediate benefits of developing an operational calendar is that it provides a full view of the year of programming ahead, which is also broken down on a monthly basis. This will allow you to pace both the number and nature of activities for special events throughout the course of the year. A written operational calendar also serves as an excellent reminder of what needs to be done and as a tool to evaluate what has already been done. On your electronic calendar—or in your folder system or wall chart—describe both what was planned, and what was done. This is useful for assessment, succession planning, conflict tracking, and many other purposes.

**For Your Information**

**Sample template for an operational calendar:**

**January**

- Traumatic Brain Injury Awareness Month (guest speaker)
- January 4—World Braille Day—International (bulletin board)
- Alzheimer's Awareness Month (book and e-book display in common room)
- Glaucoma Awareness Month (promotional giveaways and town ceremony)

**February**

- Heart and Stroke Month (building signage provided by Health Department)
- 1st Week—National Therapeutic Recreation Week (guest speaker and demonstration)
- February 2—Rheumatoid Arthritis Awareness Day (ribbons and display by Friends)
- February 15—International Childhood Cancer Day (book excerpt reading marathon)

**March**

- Developmental Disability Awareness Month (speaker series in common room)
- Multiple Sclerosis Month (signage and promotion of Health Center's events)
- March 21—World Down Syndrome Day (group party and recognition ceremony)
- March 25—US National Cerebral Palsy Awareness Day (bulletin board and bookcases)

**April**

- April 2—World Autism Awareness Day
- April 4—Auditory Processing Disorder Awareness Day
- April 11—Parkinson's Disease International Awareness Day
- Last Saturday in April—Show Your Mettle Day—Awareness day to encourage amputees to show their metal (prosthetic devices, wheelchairs, etc.)

**May**

- ALS Awareness Month
- Cystic Fibrosis Awareness Month
- Lupus Awareness Month
- May 7—National Children's Mental Health Awareness Day

**June**

- PTSD Awareness Month
- June 7—National Cancer Survivors Day
- June 19—World Sickle Cell Day
- June 30—Arthrogryposis Awareness Day

**July**

- Fragile X Syndrome Awareness Month
- National Cleft and Craniofacial Awareness and Prevention Month
- July 16—Disability/ADA Awareness Day
- July 28—World Hepatitis Day

*(continued on page 130)*

**For Your Information (cont'd)**

**August**
- Cataract Awareness Month
- Spinal Muscular Atrophy Awareness Month
- Stevens-Johnson Syndrome Awareness Month

**September**
- Sickle-Cell Anemia Awareness Month
- September 4—World Cerebral Palsy Day
- September 5—International Day of Charity
- September 9—International Fetal Alcohol Spectrum Disorder Awareness Day

**October**
- AIDS Awareness Month
- Disability Employment Awareness Month
- October 10—World Mental Health Day
- October 15—World Blind Day/ World Sight Day

**November**
- Alzheimer's Awareness Month
- Epilepsy Awareness Month
- Lung Cancer Awareness Month

**December**
- December 1—World Aids Day
- December 3—International Day of Persons with Disabilities
- December 10—Human Rights Day

## Signature Events for Public and Special Libraries

To avoid information overload of your staff members and patrons, try to discern which events will be your library's signature programs during the year. These will get more attention, as compared to other events; they could be more complex or involved, and they might attract outside funding. Choose one or two for which your library can be well-known in the region, and which are distinct from other organizations' events or which purposefully involve them.

Once committed to hosting a signature event, you will need to develop a planning committee to set the process in motion. Whether your signature event is for a day, a week, or a month, it will be necessary to do as much advanced planning as possible. Once you finalize your event date, the next step will be to secure partners with whom to collaborate in the community.

In choosing partners for collaboration you may want to consider inviting them to join the planning committee. Their input and contributions will prove

> ### ✔ Checklist
>
> Points to consider when planning events with partner organizations:
>
> - ☐ Planning/organizing committee members
> - ☐ Ground rules for laying out plans and taking action
> - ☐ Stakeholders to consult for input
> - ☐ Budget requests and expenditure process
> - ☐ Schedule of activities (program content)
> - ☐ Schedule of activities (room assignments)
> - ☐ Technology and equipment for the event
> - ☐ Staffing for event and for library operations during event times
> - ☐ Marketing of event, methods of advertising
> - ☐ Security and safety at event, crowd control

invaluable when deciding on locations and times for your events. Opportunities multiply when the activities of your signature event take place at many locations. Such collaborations will be mutually beneficial in promoting your event and in showcasing the venue of your cohost.

Working backwards from the event date, build in some flexible time in case something goes wrong, because things always take longer than we think they will. Build in time to complete paperwork, obtain signatures, convene board meetings, and secure grant approvals. Include time for partners to ponder your offer and for volunteers to determine the length and nature of their service.

Some of our tech-savvy colleagues use a Gantt chart to plot the many simultaneous moving parts that all have different completion dates. Other colleagues have natural talents for remembering tasks and asking good questions. Involve colleagues with all types of abilities as part of the planning process, even if they do not take active roles in the delivery of programs.

## Academic Year Cycle for Schools

College and university libraries naturally monitor their school's academic calendar closely when planning new programming for the upcoming year. While some campus facilities are easy to schedule, others may need nine to twelve months' advance notice to reserve. Working with other departments that also schedule periodic events is a necessity, because they will know what events they have planned even if they are not yet booked or contracted.

Depending on the time of year, you may decide to limit your programming during periods when students, faculty, and staff may be committed or preoccupied. This is true for other types of libraries as well; users may not be in a position to attend a workshop or activities in September if they have school-age children. The month of May is a busy and hectic time on a college campus because of finals and commencement week. However, these are also good times to preview your upcoming events, evaluate previous events, or get ideas for new events, because a critical mass of users will be nearby.

**✓ Checklist**

School events that can help you promote disability awareness:

- ☐ Commencement
- ☐ School musicals/plays
- ☐ Polling and voting events
- ☐ Holiday celebrations
- ☐ Athletic events
- ☐ PTA meetings
- ☐ Fire safety training
- ☐ Bullying training

Sometimes fixed seasonal events are the best times to host a program. During Finals Week, our university hosts an event with therapy pets. This activity appeals to students with and without disabilities who want to take breaks from studying to reduce stress. Again, library staff may not know if a student they meet has a hidden disability. An event like this would be truly inclusive and would benefit many students and staff visiting the library.

One possible event during Commencement Week may include the library hosting a reception in collaboration with Disability Resources for graduating students with disabilities. What better suitable location than the library to host an event that recognizes the academic achievements of students with disabilities, held in a place that just a few years earlier may have seemed intimidating.

Just as the Office of Disability Resources plays an important role in supporting students with disabilities at the college level, the role of the library and its staff is just as significant. A student with a disability follows a path from orientation to graduation, and has benefitted the influence of many staff members, even those behind the scenes. Graduations, award ceremonies, and honors gatherings can be unofficial awareness times when students, parents, and staff members can recognize each other for their contributions to creating success along the way.

## Disability Awareness Week/Month Programming

Most disability resource departments in higher education provide academic coaching to new students with disabilities to develop skills in the areas of self-advocacy and independence. Therefore, showing new students with disabilities the locations of key resources to their academic success on campus is critical. As students begin to frequent the library, tours are available and staff present to provide training on how to use specific equipment and software designed for persons with disabilities.

October is designated as National Employment Disability Month, which is celebrated each year by schools and community organizations throughout the country. At Rowan University, collaborations take place among faculty, staff, and student organizations that promote diversity, inclusiveness, and disability awareness across campus. Events scheduled throughout the week include diversity speakers, disability awareness movies, and interactive activities such as wheelchair ballroom dancing.

Collaborations with the Campbell Library have proved invaluable in promotions of Disability Awareness Week. The library strategically places sandwich board displays listing the schedule of events for the week at the entrance to the library. In addition, disability-themed books and movies fill the display cases in the lobby area and across from the information desk. Librarians can easily become involved in film screenings, performances, and faculty research presentations, as well as staff a table at the resource fair.

To further promote inclusive environments, the Campbell Library has hosted open houses and tours of specialized resources and facilities. Library staff provided visitors with hands-on demonstrations of new assistive technology along with computer-based tutorials and workshops on closed captioning and universal design.

Librarians and other library staff members were speakers at various events, as well as attendees. A web page with specific resources and directions for accessing electronic books and articles via screen readers was another of the library's initiatives last year to help reach the objectives of this event. Invite other departments to generate ideas for promoting awareness of disabilities.

**For Your Information**

Sample full schedule of Rowan University's programs for Disability Awareness Week

**Monday, Oct. 24**

**11:00 am–1:00 pm:** Disability awareness week kick-off event (food, drink, and music in student center)

**1:00 pm:** Ceremony: Honor three members of the Rowan community with "dedicated professional and Faculty Awards" for outstanding services to students and staff with disabilities (Commons)

**7:00 pm:** Screening of the documentary film, "Shake, Rattle and Roll," about disabilities, followed by a question-and-answer session with the Rowan student filmmakers (Auditorium)

**Tuesday, Oct. 25**

**11:00 am–12:30 pm:** Rowan alumna Laura Schwanger, a member of the US Paralympic Rowing Team, will discuss her experiences as a medal-winning athlete. (Ballroom)

**2:00 pm:** Try-on-a-Disability event. Gain knowledge about what it's like to be blind, in a wheelchair, or have a learning disability through challenging exercises presented by students and faculty members with disabilities. (Student Center)

**9:00 pm:** Tim Grill, "The Barely Can Stand-Up Comic" will perform. A professional comedian who was born with spina bifida, Grill has performed at The Comedy Store in Hollywood, among other venues. (Commons)

**Wednesday, Oct. 26**

**10:00 am–2:00 pm:** Rowan community members will have the opportunity to learn about the latest in assistive technology products to help people with disabilities during Technopalooza. (Memorial Hall, Training Rooms A and B)

**2:00 pm:** Panel: Rowan students will discuss living with disabilities. (Education Hall, Room 2098)

**8:00 pm:** Performance by Reesa and the Rooters, a '70s Flashback and '80s New Wave band. Lead singer Reesa Marchetti, who has multiple sclerosis, entertains crowds from her power scooter. (Commons)

*(continued on page 135)*

**For Your Information** *(cont'd)*

**Thursday, Oct. 27**

    **10:00 am–1:00 pm:** Resource Fair with tables designed to provide information and services to people with disabilities. (Student Center)

    **10:00 am–1:00 pm:** Rowan faculty members will present poster sessions on their work and research focusing on the disability community. (Education Hall Atrium)

    **1:30–3:30 pm:** Dancers with the American Dance Wheels Foundation will perform—and challenge able-bodied members of the Rowan community to give wheelchair ballroom dancing a try—during their second annual appearance at Rowan. (General Exercise Room, Rec Center)

    **4:00 pm:** Rowan professors Jay Kuder and Jay Chaskes will join forces to provide training to faculty members about working with students with Asperger Syndrome. (Education Hall, Room 3114)

**Friday, Oct. 28**

    **10:00 am:** "Accessibility and Your Apple Computer" will inform users how to better utilize Apple technology. (Memorial Hall, Training Room A)

    **1:00 pm:** Zarifa Roberson of the Philadelphia-based magazine i.d.e.a.1 (Individuals with Disabilities Express about Life) will discuss her work as founder of the publication. (Admissions Hall)

    **2:00 pm:** Celebrating Everyday Achievements: Panel includes people with disabilities from the community who have achieved success in sports, entertainment, and business. (Student Center)

For more information about any of the Disability Awareness Week events, contact the Academic Resource Center or visit www.rowan.edu/studentaffairs/asc.

## Communicating with and about People with Disabilities: Year-Round Programming

When deciding on programming ideas for Disability Awareness events, you may want to consider a recurring workshop on best practices for using first-person language when communicating with persons with disabilities. This comprehensive list of tips and best practices can also be the focus of a display case, a poster in a high-traffic area, or a bibliography or webliography of resources for your library home page. You can even create videos to illustrate key concepts, with some of your patrons as actors and directors.

> The Americans with Disabilities Act, other laws, and the efforts of many disability organizations have made strides in improving accessibility in buildings, increasing access to education, opening employment opportunities and developing realistic portrayals of persons with disabilities in television programming and motion pictures. Where progress is still needed is in communication and interaction with people with disabilities. Individuals are sometimes concerned that they will say the wrong thing, so they say nothing at all—thus further segregating people with disabilities. Listed here are some suggestions on how to relate to and communicate with and about people with disabilities. (http://snohomishcountywa.gov/DocumentCenter/View/20017)

---

 **For Your Information**

**These following suggestions are from the US Department of Labor's Office of Disability Employment Policy as posted on the website of the Georgia Emergency Preparedness Coalition for Individuals with Disabilities and Older Adults (http://web.gsfic.ga.gov/ADA/FNSS%20Toolkit.htm).**

Positive language empowers. When writing or speaking about people with disabilities, it is important to put the person first. Group designations such as "the blind," "the retarded," or "the disabled" are inappropriate because they do not reflect the individuality, equality or dignity of people with disabilities. Further, words like "normal person" imply that the person with a disability isn't normal, whereas "person without a disability" is descriptive but not negative.

The accompanying chart shows examples of positive and negative phrases.

*(continued on page 137)*

## ℹ️ For Your Information (cont'd)

| Affirmative Phrases | Negative Phrases |
| --- | --- |
| person with an intellectual, cognitive, developmental disability | retarded; mentally defective |
| person who is blind, person who is visually impaired | the blind |
| person with a disability | the disabled; handicapped |
| person who is deaf | the deaf; deaf and dumb |
| person who is hard of hearing | suffers a hearing loss |
| person who has multiple sclerosis | afflicted by MS |
| person with cerebral palsy | CP victim |
| person with epilepsy, person with seizure disorder | epileptic |
| person who uses a wheelchair | confined or restricted to a wheelchair |
| person who has muscular dystrophy | stricken by MD |
| person with a physical disability, physically disabled | crippled; lame; deformed |
| unable to speak, uses synthetic speech | dumb; mute |
| person with psychiatric disability | crazy; nuts |
| person who is successful, productive | has overcome his/her disability; is courageous (when it implies the person has courage because of having a disability) |

Because libraries are the meeting place for many members of the community as well as for nonprofit organizations, it is useful to provide information that a user who has time to browse can locate. When considering community partners in planning disability and diversity events, you may not have to look too far. The interested patrons may just come to you!

**For Your Information**

According to Alaska's Governor's Council on Disabilities and Special Education, "etiquette considered appropriate when interacting with people with disabilities is based primarily on respect and courtesy." Outlined below are tips to help you in communicating with persons with disabilities.

**General Tips for Communicating with People with Disabilities**

The United Cerebral Palsy Foundation offers the following advice:
- When introduced to a person with a disability, it is appropriate to offer to shake hands. People with limited hand use or who wear an artificial limb can usually shake hands.
- If you offer assistance, wait until the offer is accepted. Then listen to or ask for instructions.
- Relax. Don't be embarrassed if you happen to use common expressions such as "See you later," or "Did you hear about that?" that seem to relate to a person's disability.
- Don't be afraid to ask questions when you're unsure of what to do.

**Tips for Communicating with Individuals Who Are Blind or Visually Impaired**

- Speak to the individual when you approach him or her.
- State clearly who you are; speak in a normal tone of voice.
- When conversing in a group, remember to identify yourself and the person to whom you are speaking.
- Never touch or distract a service dog without first asking the owner.
- Tell the individual when you are leaving.
- Do not attempt to lead the individual without first asking; allow the person to hold your arm.
- Be descriptive when giving verbal directions. For example, if you're approaching steps, mention how many.
- If you are offering a seat, gently place the individual's hand on the back or arm of the chair.

**Tips for Communicating with Individuals Who Are Deaf or Hard of Hearing**

- Gain the person's attention before starting a conversation (i.e., tap the person gently on the shoulder/arm).
- Look directly at the individual, speak clearly and keep your hands away from your face.
- If the individual uses a sign language interpreter, speak directly to the person, not the interpreter.

*(continued on page 139)*

**For Your Information** *(cont'd)*

**Tips for Communicating with Individuals with Mobility Impairments**

- If possible, put yourself at the wheelchair user's eye level.
- Do not lean on a wheelchair or any other assistive device.
- Do not assume the individual wants to be pushed—ask first.
- Offer assistance if the individual appears to be having difficulty opening a door.

**Tips for Communicating with Individuals with Speech Impairments**

- If you do not understand something the individual says, ask the individual to repeat what he or she said.
- Be patient. Take as much time as necessary.
- Do not speak for the individual or attempt to finish her or his sentences.

**Tips for Communicating with Individuals with Cognitive Disabilities**

- If you are in a public area with many distractions, consider moving to a quiet or private location.
- Be prepared to repeat what you say, orally or in writing.
- Be patient, flexible, and supportive. Take time to understand the individual and make sure the individual understands you.

**Remember**

- Relax and treat the individual with dignity, respect, and courtesy.
- Listen to the individual and offer assistance but do not insist or be offended if your offer is not accepted.

A glance at your current library calendar of events and lists of community organizations who routinely reserve space in your library and neighboring libraries or facilities often helps to identify ideal partners for collaborations. These organizations also come to the planning process with an existing database of customers that they serve, or who are a vital part of their outreach efforts in the community.

For example, a 2016 article by Sean Patrick Murphy in the *Burlington County Times* newspaper tells the in-depth story of the Burlington County Library System in New Jersey. The 2,500-word article focused on the relevancy of libraries in a digital age, and was part of an ongoing series about libraries for the paper. The sheer number of community partnerships currently taking

**For Your Information**

For example, here are some of the many partners of the Burlington County (NJ) Library System:

- Workforce Development Institute
- Burlington County College
- American Historical Theatre
- New Jersey Council for the Humanities
- Educational Services/Special Services Unit
- National Endowment for the Humanities
- Rutgers Cooperative Extension
- New Jersey Coalition for Financial Education
- American Library Association
- Burlington County Juvenile Detention Center
- Free Library of Philadelphia
- Smithsonian Institute

place within the Burlington County Library System rivals those of municipal libraries operating in the county.

In his article, Murphy quotes Willingboro Municipal Library Director Christine Hill, who reports that her library "has had more than 330 organizations use its three large meeting rooms [in 2015] and over 1,300 small groups use its study rooms." Also noteworthy in the article was the reporting that "the county library system also hosts more than 3,800 programs each year, according to county information." This level of activity provides an extraordinary number of potential connections for workshop presenters, and attendees, as well as networking options. A statistic like this is proof of the fertile ground within the library's usual operations to cultivate partnerships with community members and nonprofit organizations as you consider hosting events promoting inclusiveness and diversity.

## Autism Awareness Week

Autism Awareness Week has become one of the signature events to which many libraries dedicate their time during the academic year. Along with valued campus partners such as the health department, local youth groups, or the

Council for Exceptional Children, this weeklong event continues to expand and gain traction with increased community participation. Many advocacy groups also participate in monthlong celebrations, promote designated days, or host similarly named events. Be sure to check on appropriate terminology when naming your own events or when purposefully aligning with specific groups' programs.

Typically, the kick-off event for this week at Rowan University usually begins with a "Light It Up Blue" Ceremony, highlighting local buildings that have changed their exterior spotlight bulbs from white to blue so that significant structures in town and on campus are showcased. Many participating homeowners in the neighborhood also participate by changing light bulbs on their porches or in lamps shining through windows of their houses. The particular shade of blue that marks this event is clearly indicated on the packaging for bulbs at most hardware and department stores.

Our campus ceremony takes place in the lobby of the Campbell Library, a central building that also has a high tower visible from the main road. Invited speakers make opening remarks that are followed by the precisely timed lighting of a number of buildings on campus blue to signify International Autism Awareness Day and the week of awareness that follows.

Sample events include a "Light It Up Blue Walk" cosponsored by the Student Council for Exceptional Children and the student assistants from the Disability Resources office. Rowan's Office of Orientation and Student Leader-

---

 **For Your Information**

Iconic landmarks that have participated in Autism Speaks' "Light It Up Blue" events:

- Empire State Building in New York City
- Niagara Falls in Canada
- Christ the Redeemer Statue in Brazil
- La Sagrada Familia Cathedral in Barcelona
- Great Pyramid of Giza in Egypt
- Shanghai World Financial Center in Japan
- Trafalgar Square in London
- Beijing Millennium Monument in China
- Eiffel Tower in Paris
- Sydney Opera House in Australia

ship Programs also started a "Prof Talks" series patterned after the TED Talks format. An autism-themed Prof Talk is now a recurring annual event.

To wrap up the week, Rowan's Italian American Club sponsors an autism benefit on campus that is open to the community. This semiformal event includes hors d'oeuvres, music, and dancing that includes persons of different abilities, and is well attended by many different local constituents. This event and most of the others listed here were covered by local newspaper reporters and photographers, university public relations staff, and student leaders via social media.

There are always many more ideas than anyone can execute themselves. Community libraries that wish to celebrate Autism Awareness Week may consider cohosting a resource fair, scheduling a speaker or an author, and perhaps hosting a sensory-friendly family movie. Again, connecting with community organizations can significantly increase your chances of having a truly inclusive and engaging event.

## Veterans' Week

The Office of Veteran Affairs at Rowan University recognizes Veterans' Day each November with a memorial service on campus. Over the years a Veterans' Week was established with events taking place across campus and throughout the community. In collaboration with the Campbell Library, staff helped to categorize memorabilia, promote print and electronic resources in the library's holdings about veterans, and display realia specific to veterans.

One year the list of names and photos of Rowan University alumni who served in the military was on display in the library "front and center" as patrons entered the building. The display was fitting tribute for those veterans who served, as well as a reminder that many had disabilities.

Some of these same veterans sacrificed their lives and others had their academic pursuits put on hold when they went off to serve their country. Others returned with disabilities and forged ahead, determined to start a new chapter in their lives with their return to college to complete their college degrees.

Collaboration among employees proved invaluable, allowing staff members from various offices to brainstorm, critique, and add resources to the displays. To start conversations among library visitors, often a veteran was also standing near the displays to correct students' impressions or engage in

**For Your Information**

Sample schedule of Veterans' Week activities which may create opportunities for disabilities awareness:

**Veterans' Week November 8–13**

**Monday November 8th:** Remembrance Walk Registration starts at 4:45 pm. Walk starts at 5:00 pm. Student Center Patio.

The Remembrance Walk is an event to honor all past, present, and future Veterans. Proceeds from the event will be donated to the Dombrowski Fund. Veterans with disabilities participate and talk with students and members of the community.

**Tuesday November 9th:** Awareness and a Movie 7pm Student Center Ballroom

Join us for a showing of the movie *Warrior Champions*, an inspiring story of a group of severely wounded American soldiers and their mission to compete for a spot on the 2008 Paralympic Games in Beijing.

**Wednesday November 10th:** Donation Table 10am—2pm Student Center Lobby

Items that can be donated include: handheld games, blank holiday cards, cereal, pop-tarts, pasta/macaroni, jars of sauce, baby shampoo, baby powder, white cotton socks, and more (see list). All items must be new and unopened. Items that are collected will be donated to the Military Support Group of NJ. While you are here, write out messages to send to active troops.

**Thursday November 11th:** Veterans Day Ceremony 11:30 am Campus Lawn

Local restaurant fundraiser. Proceeds go to Veteran Students Organization. Flier must be presented to your waiter/waitress for VSO to benefit from the restaurant donation.

**Friday November 12th:** Football Game 7:30pm Athletic Stadium

Baked goods sale and Toys for Tots collection box hosted by Veteran Student Organization. Veterans and their families get free admission by showing military ID.

conversation. These types of events are priceless. Tap into the talents of those with organizational skills as well as those who can eloquently communicate appropriate messages about persons with disabilities.

## Welcome Week and Creating Traditions

During the opening weeks of school in September, Rowan University's College Compass Transition Program hosts get-togethers for students and faculty to socialize before the semester is under way. Newly accepted students with disabilities move onto campus early to acclimate to the environment and connect with academic resources. Embedded in the program is a visit to the library for a tour of resources and the Digital Scholarship Center, which is equipped with designated computers loaded with assistive software for individuals with disabilities.

Shortly thereafter, the Division of Student Life sponsors "Start Up Smart" events through the first two weeks of school to help new students reinforce healthy choices as they begin their college careers. Libraries could collaborate with these types of partners by cohosting events, bringing library resources for attendees to browse, creating pathfinders, or providing demonstrations of online content such as e-books and database articles.

At the start of every fall semester, Disability Resources schedules overview workshops for new students with disabilities who are eligible for classroom accommodations. The workshop also provides valuable information about resources such as academic coaching, tutoring, the Writing Center, the Social Justice Center, the American Sign Language Club, and Delta Alpha Pi, an honor society for college students with disabilities.

In summary, the earlier the outreach, the better the outcomes. Time spent developing and documenting collaborations will result in a diverse programming schedule for the upcoming academic year. And each year's theme or slate of activities will create a new tradition for your organization, and even for your larger community. Traditions are usually shared cultural experiences that leave lasting impressions, and you never know which of your events might spark renewed interest in your constituents. Plan a variety and see what happens!

## Resources

American Library Association. 2015. "Celebration Weeks and Promotional Events." www.ala.org/conferencesevents/celebrationweeks.

Boden, Katherine, and Karisa Tashjian. 2015. "ALL Access: Adult Education and Digital Literacy for Workforce Development in Public Libraries." *Computers in Libraries* 35 (10): 26–31.

"Creative Media Projects Encourage a More Inclusive World for the Disabled." 2010. *Multimedia Information and Technology* 36 (1): 4.

DisabledWorld.com. "List of Health and Disability Awareness Days, Weeks and Months." www.disabled-world.com/disability/awareness/awareness-dates .php.

Georgia Emergency Preparedness Coalition for Individuals with Disabilities and Older Adults. "State of Georgia Functional and Access Needs Support Services Toolkit." (http://web.gsfic.ga.gov/ADA/FNSS%20Toolkit.htm).

Holmes, Paula. 2007. "A Parent's View: How Libraries Can Open the Door to the 20 Percent." *Children and Libraries* 5 (3): 24.

King, J. Freeman. 2015. "What Constitutes a Quality Program for Children Who Are Deaf?" *The Exceptional Parent* 45 (3): 42–43.

Klipper, Barbara. 2014. "Making Makerspaces Work for Everyone." *Children and Libraries* 12, (3): 5–6.

——. 2014. *Programming for Children and Teens with Autism Spectrum Disorder.* Chicago: ALA Editions.

Kuni, Kayla, and Linda Holtslander. 2015. "You Belong @ Your Library: Programming for Adults with Intellectual Disabilities." www.programminglibrarian .org/learn/you-belong-your-library-programming-adults-intellectual -disabilities.

Murphy, Sean Patrick. 2016. "Ongoing Story: County Libraries Relish Their Relevancy in the Digital Age." *Burlington County Times*, June 10, A1, A3.

REM Ohio. "Ideas for Promoting Developmental Disability Awareness." www.rem-oh.com/documents/pdf/1125_Awareness%20Activities.pdf.

Robinson, Shannon Marie. 2015. "Outsider Art: Online Sources for Research." *College and Research Libraries News* 76 (1): 43–46.

Safe Zone Project. "All Activities." http://thesafezoneproject.com/all-activities.

Smith, Mary Olive. 2014. "Libraries and Autism: We're Connected [video]." www.librariesandautism.org/video.htm.

SNAILS Special Needs and Inclusive Libraries Services Group [Chicago]. "Resources." http://snailsgroup.blogspot.com/p/resources.html.

Snohomish County, Washington. "Communicating with and about People with Disabilities." http://snohomishcountywa.gov/DocumentCenter/View/20017.

State of Alaska. Governor's Council on Disabilities and Special Education. "Hiring People with Disabilities." www.dhss.alaska.gov/gcdse/Pages/jobs/service.aspx.

Thiem-Menning, Ashley. "Library Programming for Children on the Autism Spectrum." http://docs.iflsweb.org/youth/autismprograms.pdf.

United Cerebral Palsy Foundation. "Disability Etiquette." www.ucp.org/resources/disability-etiquette.

United States Department of Labor. Office of Disability Employment Policy. "Communicating with and about People with Disabilities." www.dol.gov/odep/pubs/fact/comucate.htm.

———. "Disability Employment Policy Resources by Topic." https://www.dol.gov/odep/topics/.

CHAPTER 8

# Accessible Resources and Technologies

U SERS DEPEND ON LIBRARIES FOR ACCESS TO THE INTERNET, and many depend on recommendations of librarians to find sources that fulfill their needs. The combination of its holdings and its expertise help the library to be an ideal location for social experiences surrounding information, communication, and technology (ICT).

Libraries serve their communities in many ways through their physical, as well as technological, resources so equity of access is paramount. It is essential to ensure that digital resources, equipment, and services provide users with access to information regardless of any particular ability or disability.

The terms "adaptive technologies" or "assistive technologies" seem to be used interchangeably today, and surely new terms will arise in the future as new technology is invented. In any case, these terms currently refer to equipment and/or software that provides for greater functionality, access, and use of everyday information for users with a variety of disabilities.

Increasing access to library resources is a mission-critical goal for libraries. Likewise, advocating for all users by providing appropriate technologies is a goal for library staff in every type of library. Offering technologies that provide equal access to information will help provide a similar experience of the library for all of your users.

Just as no two humans are exactly the same, no two instances of disability are identical. Therefore, we must provide options for customization and mod-

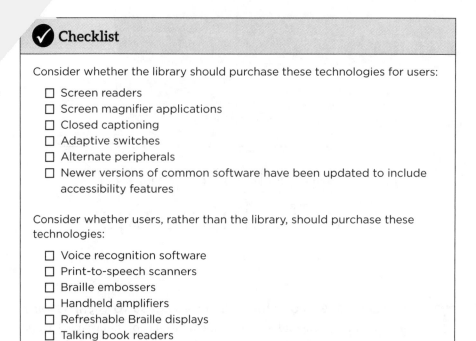

**✅ Checklist**

Consider whether the library should purchase these technologies for users:

- ☐ Screen readers
- ☐ Screen magnifier applications
- ☐ Closed captioning
- ☐ Adaptive switches
- ☐ Alternate peripherals
- ☐ Newer versions of common software have been updated to include accessibility features

Consider whether users, rather than the library, should purchase these technologies:

- ☐ Voice recognition software
- ☐ Print-to-speech scanners
- ☐ Braille embossers
- ☐ Handheld amplifiers
- ☐ Refreshable Braille displays
- ☐ Talking book readers

ification in all of our information and technological offerings. Providing good explanations of how to use the technology properly and effectively may be just as important as the equipment itself.

In our lifetime, we all may be able to experience a world where accessible modifications will be standard practice. Until then, libraries, schools, and other institutions must strive to ensure that modern technologies are available and up-to-date.

When a library fails to meet patron needs to use technology, it creates a fundamentally disappointing experience in the minds of users. This negative experience can quickly and sometimes permanently influence their perceptions about the value of the library itself. Therefore, care must be taken to prevent these problems from surfacing in the first place.

Providing equipment that enables barrier-free access to existing and emerging information and communication channels not only ensures equity, it helps all users. For example, how many of us have wished for larger print on computer screens? Or the ability to ask a quick question online without going through a half-dozen login steps? It is totally within our power to create and market many of these options that improve our users' daily lives.

**For Your Information**

Common complaints that indicate a need for universal design of your website:

- "What I wanted is not here/on the first page."
- "I can't find where to click."
- "I wish this page had more information."
- "This page is so busy, it hurts my eyes!"
- "Why would/should I click here?" often followed by "How would I have known that?"
- "This web page stinks."

Similarly, a properly coded website, just like a well-designed building layout or piece of furniture, improves the lives of its users regardless of their ability status. A key principle of web accessibility is having a website that is flexible enough in its design and presentation to meet multiple preferences of any range of users. This chapter will explore strategies for website improvement and more.

Barrier-free library technology environments address a wide range of needs at any given time. Effective websites can serve well those on a slow Internet connection or a mobile device, or those experiencing temporary disabilities or symptoms of aging, simultaneously. Nimble technologies, just like flexible physical spaces, will be able to meet the needs of all who approach them, and do so without requiring additional effort on the part of the user.

## Accessible Library Websites

Website designers and developers never really know how many of their users will have a disability. And census counts or statistics on your local community will never really identify which of those individuals will frequent your library web page. Therefore, either library users will need to self-identify and describe their problems to you, or you will simply have to assume that universal design strategies will lessen most of the problems that users encounter. Universal design makes things easier, more obvious, and more efficient. Upgrades and updates help everyone, whether those users are disabled or not.

An important aspect of library accessibility is the quality of its website. The WCAG 2.0 W3C recommendations, and its successors, give guidance on the principles of web accessibility to website creators. Specifically, websites must be accessible to a wide variety of devices including those that assist persons with disabilities. And, web content must be able to evolve with changing technologies.

For example, messages on your web page must not be conveyed solely through the use of color or graphic design. If you do use color, provide adequate color contrast whenever possible. Logical hierarchies of top-level and subordinate-level text headings, as well as an easily maneuverable and logical layout of the entire website, are truly necessary to make your site understandable to all.

Websites may benefit from use of a content management tool to reduce the number of errors resulting from automated website checkers like the previously popular Bobby, WebEXACT, WAVE and their successors. Website content management systems like Drupal or WordPress often have default structures and settings in place that may mitigate accessibility problems.

In the event that a content-management system is not available to library staff, the mere presence of skip-navigation links for enabling content that is more easily handled by screen readers is a positive indicator that a library's website is sensitive to accessibility guidelines and working toward a barrier-free experience for all users.

---

### ✅ Checklist

Are these aspects of your library website accessible via screen readers?

- ☐ Library website start page
- ☐ Website menu items and links
- ☐ Library catalog
- ☐ Article database pages
- ☐ Discovery layer tools
- ☐ Other vendor products (e-books, tutorial videos, etc.)
- ☐ Information literacy tutorials
- ☐ Subject guides and lists
- ☐ Online chat function
- ☐ Interlibrary loan directions
- ☐ Use/navigation of building directions
- ☐ Reference/help contacts

It is important to check accessible web guides, subject guides, or research guides as important components when evaluating your library website's accessibility. Some of these pages may be run by a third-party vendor like Springshare's LibGuides or by website-building modules, and so may be well-positioned to meet the types of barrier-free guidelines described above.

Website content can be tested by viewing it through multiple devices at various screen sizes and resolutions, through screen readers and alternate browsers. Check ease of use when only keyboards are used to navigate the links to main content. A page with clean HTML5 or XML, and their successors, will function well when viewed with any device.

Inadequate color contrast, confusing organization of information, and Flash-coded images or function buttons are also frequent problem areas that appear on many websites and make them unintelligible to users accessing library content through screen readers. The goal should be to ensure that all new users of your library website are able to understand and navigate your web page successfully on their first attempt.

Adjustments to web pages must not be done haphazardly when attempting to meet accessibility guidelines; in fact, changes and updates must be reviewed systematically and updated properly. Approximations of current

---

## ✅ Checklist

Some of the most common website coding errors:

- ☐ Color contrast errors
- ☐ Missing labels for form boxes
- ☐ Missing alt text for images
- ☐ Missing document language
- ☐ Empty links
- ☐ Empty buttons
- ☐ Missing alt text for buttons
- ☐ Broken skip-link navigation
- ☐ Missing alt text for spacer images
- ☐ Invalid long filename descriptions
- ☐ Empty table headers
- ☐ Marquee or scrolling text
- ☐ Automatic page refreshes or redirects

accessibility guidelines can be as damaging as not even attempting to incorporate updates. Instead, your accessibility assessments must be thorough and your implementations comprehensive. Advance planning will help to accomplish this more efficiently.

For example, some special collections libraries did not meet accessibility parameters for appropriate alternative text descriptions, which made some of their web page content inaccessible to users with disabilities. It was not enough that the libraries had taken great care in adding alt-text tags to their website content; rather, the quality of these tags was called into question as a matter of inequity. Due diligence in online design must be an ongoing, critical process of continuous quality improvement.

Some other common website barriers include: colors that contain meaningful information (e.g., all children's books listed in red and all young adult books listed in blue); low-contrast color schemes or fancy fonts that are not easy to read at first glance; multimedia without descriptive captions or transcripts; instructions that depend on spatial relationships (e.g., asking users to click something in the "left column" or "above the logo"); pop-up menus or other motion-based features of vendor-purchased services or resources; clickable graphics that are too small, that blink, or that open in new windows without notification.

Specifically, there are several ways to begin to address these website design issues. One of the primary ways is to devise an actual plan for populating a website with information, for checking for compliant coding, and for evaluating your content, layout, and updating strategies periodically. A website like ADA.gov's Accessible Technology page can help to identify where to start and how far to adjust.

Plans should include mandating frequent use of a variety of automated link checkers and tools within staff workflows, and making a commitment to conducting focus groups and user experience studies. They should also include partnering with more experienced peer institutions and individuals for advice on the best ways to approach large-scale upgrades.

Issues to consider include options for: tackling different issues in teams; prioritizing website design work and training staff; and determining benchmark goals and time lines for completion. Working together with other libraries that have gone through this process is invaluable in order to obtain context for organizing this work.

Directions to users of the library website must also be communicated in ways that make sense according to universal design principles. For example, interlibrary loan directions must be able to be read and interpreted accurately, whether the user is manipulating text on the screen by enlarging the font or colors, or by operating a refreshable Braille display.

Universally designed content and layout can only be truly accessible when all users can experience them without technical barriers. Therefore, it is important to check each and every element of each and every library web page to ensure that these types of issues will not impede users' progress toward obtaining the information that they need.

## Accessible Article Databases and Collections

Third-party vendor products like journal-article databases, serials organizing tools, and library-holdings catalogs also need to address accessibility issues. Librarians may need to contact these vendors to ask for updates and upgrades to their software to ensure that vendors are aware of how important accessibility really is. Just as we are successful in arguing for changes to the physical aspects of libraries and archives, we need to use these same arguments to argue for increased open and equitable access to the third-party online technology products we utilize.

The wealth of content collected and licensed by libraries for online access may not be intuitive to most users. Institutional and departmental priorities, politics, staff skills, privacy, and money are all real barriers to truly accessible library collections and website features. However, they are never good enough reasons to avoid addressing accessibility issues.

It is our duty as stewards of information to ensure that any process required by a database or catalog vendor is as seamless as possible technologically, is supported by good instructions, and is clearly explained to users. As more and more people with ongoing or temporary disabilities exercise their rights for accommodations under the ADA, libraries will need to become more nimble in choosing, setting up, and assisting with the accessibility features of online resources designed by others.

Finding and correcting HTML code on a library web page may be within reach of many staff members, if they are shown how to use an automated

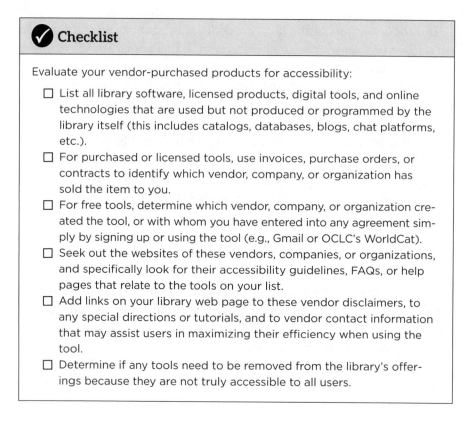

✓ **Checklist**

Evaluate your vendor-purchased products for accessibility:

☐ List all library software, licensed products, digital tools, and online technologies that are used but not produced or programmed by the library itself (this includes catalogs, databases, blogs, chat platforms, etc.).

☐ For purchased or licensed tools, use invoices, purchase orders, or contracts to identify which vendor, company, or organization has sold the item to you.

☐ For free tools, determine which vendor, company, or organization created the tool, or with whom you have entered into any agreement simply by signing up or using the tool (e.g., Gmail or OCLC's WorldCat).

☐ Seek out the websites of these vendors, companies, or organizations, and specifically look for their accessibility guidelines, FAQs, or help pages that relate to the tools on your list.

☐ Add links on your library web page to these vendor disclaimers, to any special directions or tutorials, and to vendor contact information that may assist users in maximizing their efficiency when using the tool.

☐ Determine if any tools need to be removed from the library's offerings because they are not truly accessible to all users.

tool that finds and explains inefficient coding on your pages. It may become necessary to test other online library products like e-book packages or database searches using assistive technologies to uncover barriers to effective use. Consider approaching current users of screen reader software to help test the accessibility levels when searching common library databases.

Thankfully, many integrated library systems have addressed the universal design issues related to accessible cataloging, acquisitions, and circulation modules so that both staff and patrons are able to use these systems with minimal additional adjustments. However, we must always be on alert for updates and upgrades of library software, because current versions may include these types of improvements. Other issues can be reported to vendors themselves, and many of whom are responsive to suggestions that help them to remain in compliance with the ADA.

Many academic studies have tested article database features using JAWS and Microsoft Window-Eyes screen readers in order to determine the technology's ability to find the full-text links to articles. Search within your article databases and on the web for up-to-date information on accessibility evaluations of many current library products.

## Making Accessible Features Familiar to All

Library websites must also include some information that specifically helps users with disabilities understand what the library has to offer. Similarly, clearly posted online information will help manage the expectations of users and allow them to learn which tools are and are not directly created and managed by local library staff.

Directions for accessing more complex materials, as well as informational disability services pages, must be present at or near the point of need, both online and in person. Needless to say, studies have shown that many libraries do not communicate this information well, if at all. Therefore, all types of libraries need an essential library web page that describes—in enough detail for expert researchers who happen to have print disabilities—the particular methods for accessing each of the library's electronic resources.

Most libraries will probably admit that they do not promote the existing accessible features of online databases such as spoken text and links to accessible views or alternative screen displays, or use them to their full capacity. Investigating this information, and then communicating it to users and staff, are an achievable first step for most libraries.

Particularly for K–12 students, the library should provide assistance that removes the barriers that prevent younger or newer users from working through homework easily. Screen-reader friendly directions provided on an iPod may help some patrons, as might videos that model the click sequences involved in locating and selecting appropriate articles.

Often, library staff will be tempted to do searches for students, overly mediating the process to compensate for the user's visual impairment. Instead, reference librarians can provide students who use screen readers specific in-person workshops or online tutorials on how to navigate library databases, which will provide equivalent information literacy instruction.

Users are clearly and negatively affected by the number of links on a page—too many links become both confusing and frustrating. Plus, labeling of those links can be confusing when trying to navigate, so ambiguous or erroneous pointers must be reported. Every effort must be made to work with vendors

---

**✅ Checklist**

Assisting users with technology: Do this, not that:

- ☐ Do ask users which assistive technology they would like to use for their current task (among those available at the library); don't just perform the task for them if, with some assistance, they are able to accomplish the task themselves.
- ☐ Do ask the users about their comfort or skill levels in using the technology; don't confuse a lack of skill with a lack of motivation.
- ☐ Do offer appointments with staff members to review how to operate assistive kiosks in the library, just as you would for more in-depth processes; don't allow an extended tutorial session to interfere with reference desk operations.
- ☐ Do check periodically that the equipment and online tools are working as intended; don't assume that users will be sophisticated or willing enough to help library IT staff fix problems.

---

to improve user experiences.

Making all of the pertinent pages easy to locate should be a goal for libraries of all types. Providing web pages and hardware that are easy to use will increase interest in the library's collections and promote efficiency for those who arrive at the library either physically or virtually.

## Accessibility and Vendors

Many states have legislated mandatory ADA-compliance for products purchased with public funding, so accessibility stakes can be high for businesses that sell databases, catalog-management software, and discovery-layer tools. Increasingly, software accessibility features will be dictating purchase decisions.

Therefore, purchase of products with government funds, such as buying technology with grant funding, must also be done with care. Violations of Section 504 of the US Rehabilitation Act of 1973, or of Title II of the Americans with Disabilities Act seem to occur regularly, and organizations without knowledge of these laws are susceptible to litigation.

For example, when one library had loaned Barnes and Noble NOOK e-book readers to its users, this grant-funded program became a target of a lawsuit. The type of NOOK purchased lacked text-to-speech capability, and therefore did not provide equal access to users with disabilities, prompting formal complaints from users who were not able to access the library's resources.

Similarly, another library was sued for using older Kindle Fire HDX devices in the classroom, which were not fully accessible by all. Many universities also subsequently became involved in litigation surrounding online courses, learning-management systems, and even technological tools used during face-to-face courses.

While these cases prove that many types of users are interested in information for lifelong learning, noncompliance with federal laws can and will be prosecuted. Ignorance of the law—by yourself, your employer, or your library product vendors—is therefore not an option.

A detailed look at the library's administrative settings on each of the licensed products, or at any in-house web coding related to the display of software features, will prove invaluable in moving these products toward compliance.

Where vendor videos already exist to educate users (e.g., a series of accessibility tips, or information on the limitations of a given product), librarians must provide visible links to these pages. When products fall short in meeting accessibility standards, librarians can make contact with vendors and advocate for these necessary components, a request that will ultimately help users in all types of libraries.

Not all vendors are able to make dynamic changes to products that have already been rolled out to customers. While smaller vendors may be able to transfer your phone call directly to an IT programmer, larger companies may need to bring up these issues at staff meetings or to brainstorm solutions that might impact multiple features of a product. The requested updates may even be included in versions for future release.

Librarians and technology professionals are in a strategic position to provide information that may help vendors improve their products, so ongoing advocacy and communication about product weaknesses are recommended. Your suggestions will improve access to information and to methods of retrieving that information, as well as help vendors become compliant with the law themselves.

One way to prioritize a plan for vendor advocacy is to analyze your website and third-party product activity or usage logs to determine the ways in which patrons are exploring sections of your website and via which devices. These traffic logs will need to be interpreted with a critical eye; for example, highly trafficked pages may not contain the most useful information, but may reveal problems with your navigational structure or collection holdings.

Ongoing testing of current and new features, along with systematic evaluations of other aspects of functionality of the library website is necessary to keep up to date with changes in both the users and the technologies involved.

By helping vendors meet these guidelines, you not only improve the chances that your library will be able to acquire quality software, products, and technologies, but also you increase the knowledge capital of those vendors who strongly support accessibility as a priority. By helping to increase their sales, you may also help to negotiate a discount on their product in exchange for doing so much of the troubleshooting and user testing for them!

One important issue to keep in mind is that innovation does not have to be tempered by or hindered by accessibility requirements. Sometimes, the best solution is a low-tech one.

## Accessible Information Literacy Tutorials

Many librarians record their own information literacy tutorials, posting them via links from their library website or posting them on free video streaming services like YouTube. This allows users to access step-by-step directions on how to use the library catalog or how to search library databases. Many vendors, such as EBSCO Information Services and ProQuest, also offer ready-made library tutorials that librarians can link to their home page with ease.

However, many video sources are not automatically ADA-accessible, and librarians must take steps to ensure that any content on vendors' web pages is fully accessible to everyone. For example, videos made by teachers and librarians will need transcripts of the spoken audio attached or closed-captioning scrolls added to the bottom of the video by hand using a software tool like iMovie or Windows Movie Maker. Descriptive captioning that details the movements of characters, explains which style of music is playing, or describes other aspects of the setting being shown on a video is also necessary to provide full access to the content in any video sequence.

**For Your Information**

Online resources to help you check functionality of vendor products include:

**Adobe Software Accessibility**
www.adobe.com/accessibility.html

**Apple QuickTime captioning and other assistive technologies**
www.apple.com/accessibility/osx/

**DisabilityResources.org Web Page Design**
www.disabilityresources.org/WEB.html

**Macromedia Accessibility**
www.macromedia.com/macromedia/accessibility

**National Center for Accessible Media**
http://ncam.wgbh.org/invent_build/web_multimedia/tools-guidelines

**Section 508: The Road to Accessibility**
www.section508.gov

**Trace Research and Development Center**
http://trace.wisc.edu

**Vischeck Colorblindness Simulator**
www.vischeck.com

**Vision Australia Colour Contrast Determinator**
www.visionaustralia.org/digital-access-determinator

**W3C Synchronized Multimedia Home Page**
www.w3.0rg/AudioVideo/

**W3C Web Accessibility Initiative (WAI) Testing Tools**
www.w3.org/WAI/ER/tools/

**W3Schools.com Tutorial on Cascading Style Sheets**
www.w3schools.com/css

**WebABLE**
www.webable.com

These complexities also suggest that automated speech-to-text software programs alone cannot provide the necessary quality of captions. A human editor must retain control of the look and feel of the video and purposefully include all of its contextual features in an accessible version.

Many software tools that are used for creating screencasts, such as TechSmith Camtasia or Adobe Captivate, have the functionality to render accessible versions of videos. In addition to adding captioning and a separate written transcript, it would be useful to allow users to control the speed of the video, turn captions on and off, and access descriptive narration of on-screen action.

Similar to structuring a website, main points of information literacy tutorials should be outlined with clear language in transcripts as well as in a graphic format. Necessary design features should give users the ability to skip parts of a tutorial or easily backtrack. Ideally, all video playback controls should be operational solely via keystrokes.

At a minimum, written transcripts of tutorials and videos on the library website, along with audio and video descriptions of the content of those items, should be within each library's reach right now. Lack of time to update is not an acceptable defense for not doing this; updates should begin immediately to ensure compliance with the law.

Librarians should have the basic skills required to complete these tasks, with the assistance of student helpers or technology-savvy patrons, in order to complete the process of developing and posting accessible tutorials about how to use services or resources of the library.

Adults with learning difficulties or cognitive disabilities may require simplified language rather than being given children's material; content should be presented in a form that is easy to understand yet doesn't sound demeaning.

Although the library may provide readily available free online training, it may not always match the needs of the learners. Budgeting time for learning, investigation, and production will ensure that these tasks are a priority and that projects match the actual needs of the library users who are being served.

Tutorials that employ universal design will simultaneously meet the needs of users with low vision, color blindness, hearing impairments or physical impairments. Thankfully, most commercial DVDs and professionally-produced tutorials already have built-in closed captioning for language translations, and closed-captioned versions can also be easily requested for public showings and for classroom use.

> ✔ **Checklist**
>
> Essential elements of your online videos:
>
> ☐ Captions—Include word-for-word notation of what is said on the video, which appears simultaneously at the bottom of the screen. Write these yourself, and then recruit volunteers who are skilled in using a captioning program, or outsource to a vendor.
>
> ☐ Descriptions—Provide verbal descriptions of images, scenery, and action. Embed a narrative audio track that works with screen readers and allows users to turn descriptions on or off.
>
> ☐ Video transcripts—Prepare a word-for-word transcription of what is said on the video, which appears in a separate document. Check for automated tools that will produce these directly from your audio and captions. Provide clear links to the location of each individual transcript.

Thus, libraries must recognize that the expectations for augmented versions of any video are not merely a nice accommodation for those with disabilities who request it; in fact, provision of captioning for any video item on the library web page is actually a legal requirement.

In addition, vendor products must be ADA compliant, or state entities cannot purchase them with public funds. Many video vendors have already solved this problem, as in the video tutorials from Lynda.com and Credo Reference. Other software tools or programs allow users to search for terms within the text of the captions.

## Accessible Online Chat Reference

Library users with disabilities may rely on your online chat services to have their questions answered easily and quickly. The relative anonymity of some libraries' chat services is an attractive option that often levels the playing field for users when communicating online. Greeting and closing rituals in chat lend themselves to a comfortable experience, just like other types of predictable service desk encounters.

> ### ✅ Checklist
>
> Your online information literacy tutorials should have:
>
> - [ ] Directions on how to navigate the screen tools or interface
> - [ ] Outlines or executive summaries of longer material
> - [ ] Navigation buttons that allow users to skip and return to content
> - [ ] Options for additional help via phone or chat

Research in online communication describes ways in which users compensate for the lack of visual cues; this is also similar to communicating with users via TTY (text telephone) devices.

Relationship development, self-disclosure, reassurance, and respect are important parts of chat interactions that become magnified for users with disabilities. Users of different ages or nationalities or language backgrounds may or may not understand slang, emoticons, jokes, and the like. Routines and chat scripts may be useful for structuring reference chats in order to provide a predictable type of conversation.

Written procedures for disconnecting with overly talkative users who may not have a real question, as well as procedures for reporting abuse, will help chatting staff members to make good decisions within the parameters of best practice. As in other areas of library service, consistent customer service will encourage repeat use of the library's chat services.

Librarians are able to find useful answers to questions about ADA-compliant chat tools from willing users who are able to test applications while employing a variety of assistive technologies, and from other libraries who have researched these topics before purchase.

Regional cooperatives and library consortia will be able to help compare products and prices; widely-adopted chat products may not always serve the needs of the particular users at any given library.

Often, synchronous video chat via Skype or other services may be useful for patrons who require longer time for questions and answers, or who rely on body language and visual cues for context.

This does not imply that in-person and phone reference will become obsolete, nor does it mean that print reference books will no longer be required by people with disabilities. In fact, these types of resources may become more important to users who have not yet mastered the complexities of a

**For Your Information**

A public knowledge base of common questions and answers serves multiple purposes, including:

- Helps all users learn how to construct chat or e-mail questions, and shows examples of how they will be answered
- Assists librarians in sharing answers to common questions to avoid duplication, especially for school projects
- Allows users with screen readers to be self-sufficient and provides information for perusal at their own pace
- Models appropriate methods for staff interactions and provides ongoing professional development

screen reader, or who cannot type due to physical limitations, and would rather talk to a human or flip through pages of a printed book than struggle online.

Video resources in multiple formats will also still serve the needs of users with low literacy in addition to other disabilities. Of course, the age of the users must also be considered. Teens may want to text-message the library instead of using these other methods, and this preference may not be at all related to their disabilities.

## Assistive Technologies and Wireless

Many additional resources on assistive technologies are available that detail best practices, so only a few current practices will be addressed here. Avatars, apps, and cloud-based software are recent developments important to libraries.

While a library may not always need to be on the cutting edge of innovation, managers should take steps to ensure that the library's technologies are keeping a reasonable pace with that of their users' outside lives. Computer operating systems and web browsers that feature accessibility functions should be assessed, and upgrades budgeted periodically, to ensure functionality of new technologies.

Libraries can also suggest apps for disabled students, and allow parents to preview them on shared library tablets before purchasing them. While this may be slightly out of the library's comfort zone, and may be more about the technologies that users bring into the library with them, it still has potential to align with the library's educational mission.

Apps for social skills, conversation practice, and concept identification are categories that may possibly interest patrons. Librarians can suggest appropriate apps and games for children and teens, for language learners, for those with developmental disabilities, or for teachers and caregivers.

The possibilities for experimentation with mobile applications are endless. Therefore, it is important to review the identified objectives of any new project to ensure that its goals align with the core purpose of the library's mission.

Yet common hardware items in libraries have started to include unique peripherals that are not easily available in consumer electronics stores. Scanners, various styles of mouse pointers such as those with gel buttons or trackballs, a choice of speakers or different styles of earphones, and the like may need to be ordered online.

Lightweight and portable devices such as tablets and laptops, or peripherals with sensing capabilities and multi-input capabilities (e.g., the ability to connect plunger-style pointers or game-controller headgear), can also be offered as alternatives to workstations. And of course, the sufficient bandwidth to handle all of these activities should be an ongoing upgrade for any library.

The needs of people with disabilities may be overlooked when a town or library goes wireless. Similarly, many users may not own computers, not know how to connect their devices to the wireless points without assistance, or may not be sure where to seek help on these issues. A full implementation would include strategies to address all of these information and communication technology needs.

Often unintentionally, many of our professional decisions about wireless access create additional layers of complexity for disabled users. A full analysis of roll-out strategies, marketing, and testing must always include users with a variety of challenges in order to properly troubleshoot network accessibility and ease of use. This will also ensure that the main objective of widespread Wi-Fi—providing free or low-cost access to those impacted by the digital divide—is wholly successful, not just for some users or for some of the time.

Sensitivity to needs of the disadvantaged or disenfranchised must be explicitly considered in planning and implementing Internet access projects in any library. Sometimes the location of wireless coverage or the range of signal strength may disproportionately affect people with disabilities.

**For Your Information**

Examples of vendor lists for finding adaptive and specialty gear:

**Perkins Library, MA**
www.perkins.org/services/other/directory/adaptive-technology-vendors

**Assistive Technology of Ohio**
www.atohio.org/vendors.html

**New York Institute for Special Education**
www.nyise.org/vendors.htm

**Jim Lubin's Makoa Listing of Vendors**
www.makoa.org/computers.htm

Good practice in planning and evaluation includes checking to ensure that all neighborhoods in town have similar access, and that use of private funding partners does not diminish the municipality's ability to make the appropriate decisions that enable servicing all users. As librarians keep up-to-date with new technologies and new applications of existing technologies for library users with disabilities, connections can be formed and a culture of technological inclusiveness will be promoted.

## Alternatives to Printed Text

An important mission of the library should be to promote full participation by providing barrier-free resources for all users. When fulfilling this mission, remember that children often need special attention so that their library experience of print materials is similar to that of their nondisabled peers. A positive association with books, reading, and libraries can be an invaluable experience for young disabled learners.

DAISY (Digital Accessible Information System) standards, for example, allow for human or computerized reading of books, which are often synchronized with text files of fiction or nonfiction materials. These guidelines ensure that users with print disabilities can access texts easily and in any combination of formats they desire. DAISY standards are easily found online, and address XML code, digital talking books, modular extensions for mathematics, skippable content structures, and accessible e-pubs and wikis, among other things.

Adjusting the speed at which a scanned text is read is particularly useful for people with visual disabilities because this allows the software to adapt to users' equipment proficiency, as well as to their reading levels. In addition, augmented text can also help struggling readers with processing issues.

A variety of equipment is available from regional and state agencies and from the National Library Service for the Blind and Physically Handicapped. Users who are familiar with Braille or who are blind and rely on audio will often already be registered for services.

Users may bring their own equipment (e.g., a laptop with a microphone, a small note-taker keyboard, or even a slate and stylus). Alternately, they may return home to use other equipment or services that help translate any materials of their choice into refreshable or embossed Braille, saved or streaming audio files, or a combination of these formats.

Making books accessible increases their value for everyone, regardless of the type of user challenge. For example, different formats and materials will appeal to users with a vision impairment, learning-based language difficulties, or issues related to aging or temporary disability. If formats are difficult to access or frustrating to read and enjoy, users will forget that they are available. Related issues to consider include the release of accessible editions of new books, the ease with which users can access materials when and how they choose, and the use of accessible methods to publicize library materials and services.

## When Low-Tech May Be the Best Tech

School and public librarians can be invaluable resources when children learn to read and are eligible to initially register for these accessibility services. Often, the school district must make arrangements to have school assignments translated into Braille or audio-recorded depending on a student's needs. Not every activity needs to become a computer activity.

Librarians should ensure that a choice of pleasure-reading titles, with Braille or audio clip previews or tactile equivalents, are also available for students so that children may fully participate in story times, select books when their class visits the library, or browse at their leisure.

While fully accessible titles will need to be ordered via the government services to which each student is subscribed, such as the National Library Service, librarians can participate by helping to create accessible booktalk materials, embossed-text promotional materials, or homemade audio clips that stay within fair-use guidelines.

Library staff members are usually able to help meet the needs of a broad range of print disabilities. In the process, they may even fulfill the preferences of nondisabled users as well. Librarians and technologists can work together to develop even more new tools—anything from adaptive mouse pointers to software that generates descriptive text from images. Few may realize the innovative and creative solutions that librarians can devise.

Library staff are able to track common questions which create frustration for users. For example, creating and displaying PDFs are some of the most common challenges for libraries and their users. The technology to create accessible PDFs—which can be read by screen readers and which clearly describe the data entry fields being requested on forms—is currently available but has not yet been widely adopted.

Both people with and without disabilities have experienced the frustration of not being able to procure a fill-in version of a PDF form, so this is an area in which a concerted effort by staff would result in a most appreciative audience. Updating staff skills—along with acquiring the appropriate software licenses that allow creating and posting accessible PDFs—is clearly a long-overdue professional-development initiative for many libraries.

An institution that fails to provide accessible websites may irreparably harm both its own reputation and that of its parent organization, school, or town. Full participation of people with disabilities in ways that do not require

---

### ✅ Checklist

Try these low-tech accessibility solutions:

- ☐ Colored films
- ☐ Square plastic magnifier sheets
- ☐ Magnifying glasses
- ☐ Handheld monocles
- ☐ Flashlights or table lamps
- ☐ Larger print on display screens and signage

their physical presence is an important goal for all organizations, not just libraries.

Barrier-free access ensures that users with a disability are able to contribute and participate just as their nondisabled peers do. Providing the same or equal opportunities for persons with disabilities to access the library's collections and services—which are, after all, paid for by their tax dollars—remains an essential function that requires attention and vigilance.

Access to networked and wireless computer access is becoming more of a fundamental human right in our country and many others. So providing appropriate resources and technologies becomes a service that is essential in helping people feel connected.

Our society is at its most effective when technology helps to level the playing field of life for users of all abilities. Librarians traditionally have been, and will continue to be, strong advocates on all of these issues.

## Resources

Abraham, Tony. 2015. "What Other Cities Should Learn from Philly's Failed Municipal Broadband Effort." (May 14). technical.ly/philly/2015/03/04/cities-learn-phillys-failed-municipal-broadband-effort.

Atkinson, Matthew Tylee, and Jatinder Dhiensa. 2007. "Improving Library Services to People with Print Disabilities: The Role of Technology in Public Libraries." In *Improving Library Services to People with Disabilities*, edited by Courtney Deines-Jones, 1–20. Oxford, UK: Chandos Publishing.

Baker, Paul M. A., Jarice Hanson, and William N. Myhill. 2009. "The Promise of Municipal Wi-Fi and Failed Policies of Inclusion: The Disability Divide." *Information Polity: The International Journal of Government and Democracy in the Information Age* 14 (1): 47–59. doi:10.3233/IP-2009-0171.

Billingham, Lisa. 2014. "Improving Academic Library Website Accessibility for People with Disabilities." *Library Management* 35 (8/9): 565–81. doi:10.1108/LM-11-2013-0107.

Brinck, Tom, Darren Gergle, and Scott D. Wood. 2002. *Designing Websites That Work: Usability for the Web*. New York: Morgan Kaufmann.

Carey, Kevin. 2007. "Library Services to People with Special Needs: A Discussion of Blind and Visually Impaired People as an Exemplar." In *Improving Library Services to People with Disabilities*, edited by Courtney Deines-Jones, 21–43. Oxford, UK: Chandos Publishing.

Cassner, Mary, Charlene Maxey-Harris, and Toni Anaya. 2011. "Differently Able: A Review of Academic Library Websites for People with Disabilities." *Behavioral and Social Sciences Librarian* 30 (1): 33–51. doi:10.1080/01639269.2011.548722.

Comeaux, Dave, and Axel Schmetzke. 2013. "Accessibility of Academic Library Websites in North America: Current Status and Trends (2002–2012)." *Library Hi Tech* 31 (1): 8–33. doi:http://dx.doi.org/10.1108/07378831311303903.

DAISY Consortium. "Specifications." www.daisy.org/specifications.

Davis, Lora J. 2012. "Providing Virtual Services to All: A Mixed-Method Analysis of the Website Accessibility of Philadelphia Area Consortium of Special Collections Libraries (PACSCL) Member Repositories." *The American Archivist* 75 (1): 35–55.

Dermody, Kelly, and Norda Majekodunmi. 2011. "Online Databases and the Research Experience for University Students with Print Disabilities." *Library Hi Tech* 29 (1): 149–60. doi:10.1108/07378831111116976.

Ellis, Katie, and Mike Kent. 2011. *Disability and New Media*. New York: Routledge.

Fairweather, Peter, and Shari Trewin. 2010. "Cognitive Impairments and Web 2.0." *Universal Access in the Information Society* 9 (2): 137–46. doi:10.1007/s10209-009-0163-2.

Francoeur, Stephen. 2001. "An Analytical Survey of Chat Reference Services." *Reference Services Review* 29 (3): 189–204. doi:10.1108/00907320110399547.

Fulton, Camilla. 2011. "Web Accessibility, Libraries, and the Law." *Information Technology and Libraries* 30 (1): 34–43.

Hall, Valerie, Suzanne Conboy-Hill, and Dave Taylor. 2011. "Using Virtual Reality to Provide Health Care Information to People with Intellectual Disabilities: Acceptability, Usability, and Potential Utility." *Journal of Medical Internet Research* 13 (4). doi:10.2196/jmir.1917.

Henry, Shawn Lawton, and Participants of the Education and Outreach Working Group, eds. 2005. "What is Web Accessibility?" www.w3c.org/WAI/intro/accessibility.php.

Hoffelder, Nate. 2012. "Sacramento Public Library Settles with DOJ over Inaccessible Nook eReaders." The Digital Reader, August 30. http://the-digital-reader.com/2012/08/30/ sacramento-public-library-settles-with-doj-over-inaccessible-nook-ereaders.

Jacobi, Laura. 2004. "Chatting at Gallaudet." *Library Journal* 129, 3.

Joly, Karine. 2011. "Web Accessibility: Required, Not Optional: Why Everybody's Talking about Accessibility and How to Move toward Compliance." *University Business* 14 (8): 31–32.

Kerkmann, Friederike, and Dirk Lewandowski. 2012. "Accessibility of Web Search Engines. Towards a Deeper Understanding of Barriers for People with Disabilities." *Library Review* 61 (8–9): 608–21. doi:10.1108/00242531211292105.

Klipper, Barbara. 2013. "Apps and Autism." *American Libraries* 44 (6): 36–39.

Kowalsky, Michelle. "Accessibility Tips for Library Articles, Databases, and Books." Rowan University. http://libguides.rowan.edu/accessibility.

Lyttle, Melanie A. 2014. "Technology in Children's Programming: Apps for Children with Special Needs." *Children and Libraries: The Journal of the Association for Library Service to Children* 12 (2): 34–35.

Maatta Smith, Stephanie L. 2014. "Web Accessibility Assessment of Urban Public Library Websites." *Public Library Quarterly* 3 (3): 187–204. doi:10.1080/01616846.2014.937207.

Mates, Barbara T., and William R. Reed. 2011. *Assistive Technologies in the Library.* Chicago: American Library Association.

Power, Rebecca, and Chris LeBeau. 2009. "How Well Do Academic Library Websites Address the Needs of Database Users with Visual Disabilities?" *Reference Librarian* 50 (1): 55–72.

Providenti, Michael, and Robert Zai III. 2007. "Web Accessibility at Academic Libraries: Standards, Legislation, and Enforcement." *Library Hi Tech* 25 (4): 494–508. doi:10.1108/07378830710840455.

Radford, Marie L. 2006. "Encountering Virtual Users: A Qualitative Investigation of Interpersonal Communication in Chat Reference." *Journal of the American Society for Information Science and Technology* 57 (8): 1046–59. doi:10.1002/asi.20374.

Ribera, Mireia, Merce Porras, Marc Boldu, Miquel Termens, Andreu Sule, and Pilar Paris. 2009. "Web Content Accessibility Guidelines 2.0: A Further Step Towards Accessible Digital Information." *Program* 43 (4): 392–406. doi:10.1108/00330330910998048.

Riley, Cordelia. 2009. "Training for Library Patrons Who Are Hard of Hearing." *Journal of Access Services* 6 (1–2): 72–97.

Saumure, Kristie, and Lisa M. Given. 2004. "Digitally Enhanced? An Examination of the Information Behaviors of Visually Impaired Postsecondary Students." *Canadian Journal of Information and Library Science* 28 (2): 25–42.

Schaeffer, Cory. 2014. "Using New Technology to Comply with ADA Assistive Listening Requirements." *Public Library Quarterly* 33 (2): 131–44. doi:10.1080/01616846.2014.910724.

Serene, Frank H. 2008. Making Archives Accessible for People with Disabilities. Washington, DC: National Archives and Records Administration. www.archives.gov/publications/misc/making-archives-accessible.pdf.

Shadiev, Rustam, Wu-Yuin Hwang, Nian-Shing Chen, and Yueh-Min Huang. 2014. "Review of Speech-to-Text Recognition Technology for Enhancing Learning." *Journal of Educational Technology and Society* 17 (4): 65–84.

Sierkowski, Brian. 2002. "Achieving Web Accessibility." In *Proceedings of the 30th Annual ACM SIGUCCS Conference on User Services*, 288–91. Providence, RI: Association for Computing Machinery,

Singley, Emily. 2015. "Usable Libraries [blog]." http://emilysingley.net.

Siriaraya, Panote, Chee Siang Ang, and Ania Bobrowicz. 2014. "Exploring the Potential of Virtual Worlds in Engaging Older People and Supporting Healthy Aging." *Behavior and Information Technology* 33 (3): 283–94. doi:10.1080/0144929X.2012.691552.

Southwell, Kristina L., and Jacquelyn Slater. 2012. "Accessibility of Digital Special Collections Using Screen Readers." *Library Hi Tech* 30 (3): 457–71.

Stephen, Chris. 2009. "The New World of Accessible Editions for Older Adults." *Australasian Public Libraries and Information Services* 22 (3): 120–27.

United States Department of Justice, Civil Rights Division. 2007. "ADA Best Practices Tool Kit for State and Local Governments: Chapter 5, Website Accessibility under Title II of the ADA." www.ada.gov/pcatoolkit/chap5toolkit.htm.

———. "ADA.gov: Accessible Technology." www.ada.gov/access-technology/index.html.

University of Washington. "Accessible Technology: Resolution Agreements and Lawsuits." www.washington.edu/accessibility/requirements/accessibility-cases-and-settlement-agreements.

Valentine, Gill, and Tracey Skelton. 2009. "'An Umbilical Cord to the World': The Role of the Internet in D/deaf People's Information and Communication Practices." *Information, Communication and Society* 12 (1): 44–65.

Vision Australia. "Colour Contrast Determinator (beta)." www.visionaustralia.org/digital-access-determinator.

Web Content Accessibility Guidelines Working Group (WCAG) World Wide Web Consortium (W3C) Web Accessibility Initiative (WAI). 2008. "Web Content Accessibility Guidelines 2.0. W3C Recommendation." www.w3.0rg/TR/WCAG20.

Williams, Virginia Kay, and Nancy Deyoe. 2014. "Diverse Population, Diverse Collection? Youth Collections in the United States." *Technical Services Quarterly* 31 (2): 97–121.

Wopperer, Emily. 2011. "Inclusive Literature in the Library and the Classroom." *Knowledge Quest* 39 (3): 26–34.

Yesilada, Yeliz, Giorgio Brajnik, Markel Vigo, and Simon Harper. 2015. "Exploring Perceptions of Web Accessibility: A Survey Approach." *Behavior and Information Technology* 34 (2): 119–34. doi:10.1080/0144929X.2013.848238.

CHAPTER 9

# Developing a
# User-Centered Culture

L IBRARY ENVIRONMENTS NATURALLY TEND TO BE USER-ORIENTED
cultures. Setting a goal to create an inclusive environment for all
users may be ambitious, but may be unattainable without ongoing
assessment of your library. However, libraries can take steps to be
proactive, and can aspire to create inclusive spaces that not only embrace the
principles of universal design but also keep pace with available technology.
An organizational culture that enhances the user's digital or physical visit to
your library will foster a spirit of community.

Keep in mind that your community may also have a percentage of users
who will only have access to the Internet when visiting your library. The eco-
nomic and social barriers to Wi-Fi access for individuals with disabilities can
limit their community connections. Consider how your answers to the following questions will illustrate the importance of an inclusive library culture:

- Who are your users?
- What are their interests?
- What are their likes and dislikes?
- What motivates them to keep coming back?

Although you will ask those questions about all library users, think about how
the answers might change when you focus specifically on library users with

disabilities. A repeat library customer is probably the best testament to your user-centered culture, with recommendations from library users to others as a close second. Happy patrons usually bring along their friends or families, so any information about what needs the library can fulfill will help to publicize the library's services.

Not all library users will realize that they have particular needs, and many queries that we would describe as ill-structured questions can lead to multiple discoveries about what the library has to offer. Therefore, creating a climate that values curiosity and expressions of personal interests, and which provides opportunities for serendipity and discovery, will meet the needs of all users.

## Consider an Organizational Climate Evaluation

One way to develop a user-centered culture is to first gauge how inclusive your library environment already is before determining a course of action. One way to accomplish this is through a climate survey, organizational scan, SWOT (strengths, weaknesses, opportunities, and threats) analysis, or some other kind of environmental assessment The concept, which is similar to the satisfaction surveys we have all taken, should be designed to obtain immediate input from users about how they utilize the library. The survey could also ask the user to identify whether or not a user has a disability. As you begin the assessment process to determine to what extent your library's culture is user-centered, emphasize the concept of universal design in the survey.

Traditional printed surveys are probably easiest for surveying your in-house clientele. Keep them short and make them available at the information desk, circulation desk, and other high-traffic areas throughout the library. The library's online portal is another area you might consider placing your survey. You might place this information on the FAQ page and leave it there to function as a year-round suggestion box.

Libraries will want to develop their own questions to solicit feedback from a variety of stakeholders. There are many ways to construct these questions, so consult your libraries' resources on questionnaire design. Be sure to send the appropriate sets of questions to the correct stakeholders; they need not all answer the same set of questions.

**For Your Information**

**Sample Likert Scale Questions for a Library Climate Survey**

(Respondents are to check their levels of agreement from Strongly Agree to Strongly Disagree)

Ask your library patrons to rate the following items:

- Our library is a welcoming place for people with disabilities.
- I have a positive experience every time I come to this library.
- The library provides appropriate accommodations for patrons at workshops and events.
- The library provides appropriate accommodations for patrons on a daily basis.
- Staff members are always available to help me when I need assistance.
- Staff members who provide assistance are knowledgeable (or kind, or prompt, etc.).

Ask your library staff to rate these statements:

- Our library is a welcoming place for people with disabilities.
- We do all that we can to accommodate users who have visible and hidden disabilities.
- The library provides appropriate accommodations for patrons at workshops and events.
- The library provides appropriate accommodations for staff members with disabilities.
- The library provides appropriate programming for people with disabilities.

When conducting surveys on a college campus, one option might be to include an invitation in the daily automated e-mail sent out to students, faculty, and staff. Public libraries can also e-mail users who may have signed up for the library news, a Facebook page, the e-mail announcement list, a library blog, or even via a monthly or quarterly printed or online newsletter.

An effective climate survey will provide much more vivid and descriptive information than simply a count of daily traffic into the library or the number of visits to your website. This is why purely numerical metrics may never fully capture the library's success stories about providing quality services and resources. It is important to purposefully and systematically collect descriptions of how the library has impacted people's lives.

It is equally important to include questions on your survey that address both physical and digital access to library materials, resources, and services. Your survey results may also capture valuable data about whether the user's physical or digital visits were fruitful. Furthermore, the interactions that patrons with disabilities report will help to capture their ongoing impressions of your library. Determine if users with disabilities were successful in accessing requested materials or in following library links to the information they needed.

Librarians who are your counterparts in other libraries can also be good sources of feedback about your library and its status in your community. Requesting candid or anonymous feedback from peers is another effective way to determine the power of your library's brand in the community. If needed, request help in the form of "secret shoppers" who will try to use your library and then report on any difficulties encountered that would affect users with disabilities of all types.

Survey tools of this nature can also be an effective model for assessing trends in the patterns of library use by persons with disabilities. For instance, we found that high-school graduates with autism spectrum disorder are tran-

 **For Your Information**

Ask these questions of fellow librarians for assistance in evaluating and planning:

- Does our library have a good reputation for providing inclusive services for people with disabilities?
- Does our library website appear to be compliant with best practices of universal design?
- Can you name any programming or partnerships that our library has offered in partnership with other organizations?
- What features of a library building, environment, or staff would you recommend as essential for serving people with disabilities?
- What other libraries, businesses, or organizations in our region would you recommend as examples of effective service to persons with disabilities?
- Where would you search to find more information about serving users with disabilities in libraries?

**For Your Information**

Ask library users for assistance in evaluating and planning by soliciting feedback about their

- Opinions of the quality of library space, programs, and services (separate adult, teen, and children's services questions as appropriate)
- Reasons for coming to the library (you may want to list the most common responses as checkbox options or use a blank box into which respondents can write or type in additional responses)
- Reasons for using the library website (with a range of options that also includes simple things like determining hours of operation or getting help with research for my term paper)
- Perceptions of what libraries should do (e.g., help people find jobs, provide space for community groups, etc.)
- Ranking of the library as a source of information or advocacy as compared with other types of organizations
- Views of the services that your library doesn't offer, or if new ones are being implemented successfully
- Concerns about the future of life, and about your library specifically

sitioning to college every year at a significant rate. At Rowan University, the number of students with autism spectrum disorder registered with the Disability Resources Office increased from twelve to seventy in the last eight years.

Consulting a disability-resources professional can be a useful strategy for any library. Even when simply using your current resources, it can be very helpful for libraries to find a method to assess the preferences and interests of users with all disabilities (e.g., ADHD, auditory processing disorders, or print disabilities). Numbers of users with specific disabilities will change over time, and this means that library resources and technologies will also need to change. In addition, you will learn about the common perceptions and misconceptions of your users as you learn more about their interests and abilities.

One significant example of a climate survey can be found easily online. The Illinois State Library embarked on an ambitious statewide survey about autism spectrum disorder (ASD) via a grant from the Institute of Museum and Library Services. This project attempted to survey the stakeholders from the entire state of Illinois about their impressions of how users with autism are

---

### ✔ Checklist

Ask your library patrons specific types of questions that help to differentiate the types of information you seek, either about their library use or their library perceptions:

- ☐ How often do you visit this library?
- ☐ Which types of items do you check out the most (children's fiction, DVDs, etc.)?
- ☐ What program or workshop topics should we consider in the future?
- ☐ How often do you leave this library with all of your questions answered?
- ☐ Which library services are most important to you (story time, reference, interlibrary loan, etc.)?
- ☐ What were the best and worst experiences you had at this library in this calendar year?

---

treated by libraries and other partner organizations. The Illinois online survey asked users about their roles and relationship to ASD issues and about the role of libraries in helping with needs, priorities, and interests around ASD. Users' answers to fifty "library use" and "library perception" questions helped to guide libraries throughout Illinois in their delivery of service

While your evaluation does not need to be quite as comprehensive, it should be targeted. Early on in your process, determine who will be surveyed, how, and how frequently these parameters must be assessed. This will ensure that users do not experience "survey fatigue" by receiving too many questionnaires in the same time period.

Can't undertake a huge survey? Then consider creating an inclusive checklist. It may be advantageous to develop a checklist of items to review when striving to establish a user-centered culture. In addition to compiling a list confirming areas where your library is already inclusive (e.g., by looking at the physical building and online access), you will be able to identify additional areas that may need improvement.

Your checklist will be a blueprint for change—a plan for addressing areas where access may be lacking for users with specific disabilities. Perhaps your checklist will simply reveal physical obstacles preventing full access at the entrance of your library. But more likely, any type of investigation that you do will provide a periodic checkup of all of your essential services as you try to look at them in new ways and from the users' point of view.

## Review Your Marketing Materials

When reviewing your current marketing materials, it is important to determine if they are accessible for users with and without disabilities. With this in mind, it is easy to see how designing an online brochure in multiple formats and with accessible features will benefit the diverse number of users that connect with your library. By following the principles of universal design, you will be able to increase access to your marketing materials, your service and resource brochures, and even your new and existing books announcements.

For instance, large print books, while perhaps intended for elderly users with declining eyesight, also benefit many users with visual impairments and possibly others with hidden disabilities such as memory disorders, post-concussion syndrome, or chronic migraines. These users may prefer large-print options. You may never know how many users you assist by offering these options. Also, you may not really know if the user is discovering large-print options in the library via its website or through other portals.

Providing a fully accessible library website is an ongoing task that requires more than regular maintenance. Fortunately, the WCAG 2.0 accessibility standards and guidelines provide a blueprint for reviewing areas of your website that help with marketing. Because new website features and new standards are constantly being introduced, it is important to keep up to date through periodic reviews so that your website remains accessible and also looks modern.

If you need assistance in making changes to your website, you may not have to look that far for advice. Do you have any colleagues in your organization or community who work in information technology or public relations? It may require a bit of relationship building, but they may be willing to answer

---

### ✓ Checklist

Ways to promote user-centered marketing materials:

☐ Make your materials available in multiple formats.
☐ Recruit users with disabilities to review drafts of marketing materials.
☐ Recruit employees with disabilities to review strategies.
☐ Recruit volunteers with disabilities to review media choices.
☐ Recruit disability organizations in your community to review drafts of fliers, announcements, or web pages.

your questions or to help with coding or graphic design. Relationships with an IT or advertising professional who is knowledgeable about WCAG 2.0 will provide opportunities for ongoing conversations about your shared goals. Even if you need to hire experts or marketing consultants, the time spent finding and working with them will be repaid when you see an increase in compliments (or a decrease in complaints) from your users.

## Review Accessibility of Your Website

While going through the stages of developing a user-centered culture, don't overlook the valuable help your users can offer for improving your website. You can recruit users with specific disabilities to log on to your website to provide feedback on accessibility. For example, a user with a visual impairment can spend time evaluating your pages and report how easy or difficult it is to navigate the entire site, including any third-party products to which you link (e.g., article databases or audiobook catalogs).

At Rowan University, the Disabilities Resources office assisted Rowan University's Web Services department to identify two students with visual impairments to review the University website. Members of the Web Services group were most appreciative of the feedback from these students, and they have made a practice of recruiting students with disabilities on an ongoing basis to review the accessibility of their website as changes are implemented.

One result of the students' review of the new website revealed that the addition of bells and whistles can be a distraction or obstacle to users who are blind. For instance, these users attempted to navigate the home page while a dynamically generated rotation of stories with photos and messages flashed across it. Although potentially entertaining for users without visual or attention disabilities, this feature made navigation difficult for users who are blind or have low vision and use JAWS screen reader software.

Having the option to revert back to an older version of the home page may prove to be the solution for users with visual impairments. Everyone needs to have full access to your website—specifically, to the entirety of your library's website, not just the home page. Ensuring that web browsing is a seamless interaction for everyone requires advance planning and group discussions about the potential effects of web features and coding decisions.

---

### ✓ Checklist

Ways to promote user-centeredness on your web pages:

☐ Place an accessibility statement on library home page.
☐ Include contact information on the home page for library support staff and the help desk.
☐ Offer multiple options to contact library support staff or the help desk (e.g., e-mail, phone, text).
☐ Provide access to the alternate home page that is clearly displayed on the website.
☐ Ensure flexibility in website navigation for users with visual impairments.
☐ Display an easy way to report problems, broken links, or coding suggestions.

---

In 2014, the Baltimore County Public Library partnered with undergraduates at Towson University who were majoring in computer science. The project was to evaluate its library services for users with print disabilities. The program evaluation and findings focused on five areas: a) web accessibility and maintenance; b) staff awareness and training; c) physical environment of the library; d) library offerings, including databases, materials, and equipment; and e) marketing materials.

The team effort identified accessibility barriers for users with print disabilities and made recommendations for improving access. The key to the evaluation of the accessibility of library services was the involvement of a Towson doctoral student with a visual impairment. As a user with a disability, details of her firsthand experience were instrumental in evaluating existing services and providing further suggestions that would help all students.

Many libraries will conclude that having many, or even a majority, of materials available in digital formats is the best way to serve users with visual disabilities, because they can access e-books and online articles through a screen reader. Such a benefit truly promotes a user-centered culture and gives users with print disabilities multiple options for access. However, many users with and without disabilities, such as older users, may find those same digital materials cumbersome or difficult to read. Those without Internet access at home are unable to make efficient use of your online-only materials, if they are able to access them at all. These reasons among many others help to explain why a balanced collection of print and digital materials will be necessary for the foreseeable future.

## Review Your Social Media Strategy

Most libraries value and include social media when crafting an outreach strategy. Connecting via online social tools will help libraries and their staff members to stay connected with users in the community. Active and vibrant library Facebook pages and Twitter messages can provide many opportunities to stay current and at the same time alert users to news and events in a timely fashion.

Just as your website's URL is listed on your printed library materials, it would be advantageous to add some content from your website like news or photos to your social media pages. You may also want to consider having the e-mail signatures of your library staff include a link to your library website as well as to the current social media services associated with your library.

Effective utilization of social media also allows your users to provide valuable feedback. Use of popular social-media tools shows your tech-savvy users that your library is relevant to their lives. With one click, users can show their approval for your posts about current news, upcoming events, or new resources. The digital connection that libraries have with users in the community is key to reaching a large segment of your customer base. In addition, sharing on social media will help to attract new users.

---

### ✔ Checklist

Ways to promote user-centered social media:

- ☐ Explore multiple social media sites (Facebook, Twitter, etc.).
- ☐ Consider joining LinkedIn and Google Groups.
- ☐ Embed library and community resources as well as relevant links in your various social media accounts.
- ☐ Establish a library You Tube channel for information and tutorials.
- ☐ Make your presentations (PowerPoint presentations and webinars) available via the library's social media accounts.
- ☐ Post or link to your forms on library social media outlets.

At Rowan University, many departments in our Division of Student Life use a social media site that we call ProfLink. The site has become an excellent vehicle to promote current and future events on campus and in the community. This method of engagement could also follow students after they graduate, as well as those alumni who become the parents of their own college students.

To attract new users, departments simply send out invitations to students, faculty, and staff. If they accept, they are added to the roster of the group's ProfLink page and are notified about newly posted photos, event announcements, and news. While similar to a Facebook page, ProfLink is capable of promoting events exclusively to those on their roster, and also of circulating other events to the community at large. Library outreach coordinators might consider using this tool to share information on current and upcoming events as a perk for connecting with the library online.

## Match Activities to Users' Needs and Interests

Although there may be many reasons that users frequent the library, the number one reason for a visit to your website or a trip to your library building is to search for resources. With this in mind, consider how to make this essential function more attractive, seamless, and stress-free.

How important is it to your organization that users with disabilities have equal access? Any diplomatic and ethical person will have to admit that this is very important. Appropriate accommodations not only will bring users with disabilities to visit your library for the first time, but also will encourage them to return time and time again. This logic is clearly parallel to that used by retail stores and restaurants—if new customers (no matter who they are or what characteristics they possess) have a good experience somewhere, they are likely to become repeat customers.

When discussing available library resources, don't limit your comments to information about how to find books, movies, or articles. Include other resources your library offers, including in-house workshops, program themes and celebrations, and events cohosted with library partners in the community. Designate a resource area within the library with a bulletin board or a kiosk so that this information is always available to help users stay informed about the spectrum of available resources the library offers.

> ### ✓ Checklist
>
> Library attributes that patrons value:
> - ☐ Cheerful staff; someone to talk to, especially about reading
> - ☐ Problem-solving via people or resources
> - ☐ A clean, well-lit environment to study
> - ☐ Fast computers and Internet access
> - ☐ A place to browse and discover new interests
> - ☐ An environment that feels like a home away from home

Keep in mind that that every library user has a unique opinion of which library resources or services are most important. In other words, users' views will vary greatly when you ask about what they value most as a feature or a benefit of the library. For some users with disabilities, the most valuable library resource may simply be a community room where their organization can hold monthly meetings.

We have all witnessed tutoring sessions taking place in our libraries—tutoring space is often rated as a valued aspect of the library. The individual being tutored may be a person with a hidden disability, an adult with a learning disability related to math, a person who never learned to read who is working with a literacy volunteer, or a high-school student who is meeting with a tutor to prepare for SAT or ACT tests. Library staff should be knowledgeable about the tutor-student relationship in order to help troubleshoot problems or to encourage further library exploration.

The library may indeed be everything to everyone, but it will also meet only some of the needs of only some of the people. Trips to the library by users with disabilities can be significantly enhanced by designating computers equipped with assistive software and having library staff on hand to answer questions, provide technical assistance, and conduct equipment demonstrations as needed. Such resources often result in the user having a positive and rewarding library experience, especially if you provide services that surprise and delight users while still remaining within the scope of the library's mission.

Community libraries frequently offer adult education courses and workshops on topics such as computer literacy or the basics of using an iPad. In striving to keep current and foster a user-centered culture, such programs like these are great opportunities to provide services to senior citizens, many of whom may also have physical or hidden disabilities.

## Involve People with Disabilities in Your Strategic Planning

As you take inventory of all of the possible ways to match resources to users' needs, be sure to include your librarians and staff who are there to assist users throughout the day, as well as those who respond to online inquiries from your website and social media sites. Use existing resources to highlight for others the principles of universal design, to teach about hidden disabilities, and to promote the talking e-book features of your library catalog or your library's computer equipment.

Once you conduct your climate survey and analyze your results you should have a clearer path as you begin the process of strategic planning for the next year. Because strategic planning isn't a "one size fits all" approach, libraries will want to consider the unique needs, preferences, and trends of their users while fostering a user-centered culture.

University libraries may want to survey faculty on campus to stay current about any published books in the areas of access, diversity, and inclusion. As those books become available, plan to offer them in an accessible digital format if possible.

---

### ✓ Checklist

Ways to promote an inclusive user-centered culture:

- ☐ Develop an accessibility advisory committee.
- ☐ Provide accessible kiosks throughout library.
- ☐ Provide signage for assistive technology areas.
- ☐ Provide signage for the location of large-print items.
- ☐ Offer study rooms for users with sensory issues.
- ☐ Plan inclusive events with community partners.
- ☐ Recruit employees with disabilities.
- ☐ Recruit volunteers with disabilities.
- ☐ Offer consultations with staff for one-on-one instruction.
- ☐ Create accessible instructional tutorials.

When striving to maintain a user-centered culture in libraries, it is recommended that user feedback be solicited on an ongoing basis in addition to scheduled yearly assessments. Keep in mind that over time both internal and external influences may change your focus. Remember to reassess previous efforts, even if they are going well, so that you can verify that time and money are spent effectively.

Many events may serve as a catalyst for your organization to begin a strategic look at its library services: a new hire with a disability may need a workplace accommodation; an influx of students with specific disabilities may require the library to purchase additional adaptive equipment or assistive technology; or users with disabilities who may not have previously utilized the library's resources or services may return and become regular customers. Being ready to respond when and where the opportunities present themselves is, as they say, priceless.

## Resources

Baker, Paul M. A., John C. Bricout, Nathan W. Moon, Barry Coughlan, and Jessica Pater. 2013. "Communities of Participation: A Comparison of Disability and Aging Identified Groups on Facebook and LinkedIn." *Telematics and Informatics* 30 (1): 22–34.

Baker, Paul M. A., Alea M. Fairchild, and Jessica Pater. 2010. "E-Accessibility and Municipal Wi-Fi: Exploring a Model for Inclusivity and Implementation." *International Journal of Information Communication Technologies and Human Development 2* (2): 52–66.

Bowman, Cynthia Ann, and Paul T. Jaeger. 2004. *A Guide to High School Success for Students with Disabilities*. Westport, CT: Greenwood Publishing.

Fidel, Raya. 2000. "The User-Centered Approach: How We Got Here." In *Saving the Time of the Library User through Subject Access Innovation: Papers in Honor of Pauline Atherton Cochrane*, Champaign, IL: Publications Office, Graduate School of Library and Information Science: 79–99.

Helgoe, Laurie. 2008. *Introvert Power: Why Your Inner Life Is Your Hidden Strength*. Naperville, IL: Source-books, Inc.

Holmes, Jennifer L. 2008. "Patrons with Developmental Disabilities: A Needs Assessment Survey." *New Library World* 109 (11/12): 533–45.

Illinois State Library. "Illinois Libraries and Autism Spectrum Disorders Stakeholder Alignment Survey." https://www.cyberdriveillinois.com/ departments/library/libraries/targeting-autism-survey.html.

Kotter International. "Kotter's 8-Step Process for Leading Change." www.kotter international.com/the-8-step-process-for-leading-change.

Laux, Lila F., Peter R. McNally, Michael G. Paciello, and Gregg C. Vanderheiden. 1996. "Designing the World Wide Web for People with Disabilities: A User Centered Design Approach." In *Proceedings of the Second Annual ACM Conference on Assistive Technologies*, Vancouver, BC, April 11–12, 94–101. New York: Association for Computer Machinery.

Lazar, Jonathan, and Irene Briggs. 2015. "Improving Services for Patrons with Print Disabilities at Public Libraries: Moving Forward to Become More Inclusive," in Brian Wentz , Paul T. Jaeger, and John Carlo Bertot (eds.). *Accessibility for Persons with Disabilities and the Inclusive Future of Libraries* (Advances in Librarianship, Vol 40), 11–32. Bingley, UK: Emerald Group.

Mayo, Kathleen, and Ruth O'Donnell. 1994. *The ADA Library Kit: Sample ADA-Related Documents to Help You Implement the Law.* Chicago, IL: Association of Specialized and Cooperative Library Agencies.

Nord, Leslie Lea. 2014. "Reaching Out: Library Services to the Developmentally Disabled." *Public Libraries Online* 53 (5): 28–32.

Oluwalola, Felicia K. 2015. "Effect of Emotion on Distance e-Learning: The Fear of Technology." *International Journal of Social Science and Humanity* 5 (11): 966–70.

Snow, Kathie. "To Ensure Freedom, Inclusion, Respect for All, It's about Time to Embrace People First Language." www.sccoe.org/depts/students/ inclusion-collaborative/Documents/Person-First_Language_Article.pdf.

Usability Net. "Key Principles of User-Centered Design." www.usabilitynet.org/ management/b_design.htm.

W3C. "Developing a Web Accessibility Business Case for Your Organization: Overview." https://www.w3.0rg/WAI/bcase/Overview.html.

Wentz , Brian, Paul T. Jaeger, and John Carlo Bertot (eds.). *Accessibility for Persons with Disabilities and the Inclusive Future of Libraries (Advances in Librarianship, Vol 40).* Bingley, UK: Emerald Group.

# CHAPTER 10

# Keeping Up to Date

T HE LIBRARY PROFESSION HAS BEEN QUITE SUCCESSFUL OVER time in keeping up-to-date with new technologies and trends in librarianship and in related fields like computer science, education, or management. Keeping informed about disability services and guidelines is an ongoing task. Too often, it is easy to forget many of the philosophical and foundational tenets of the library's mission while preoccupied by day-to-day activities. Disability awareness is truly a topic of lifelong learning, and the more you know, the better your library services will become.

Library environments always benefit from staff awareness of current issues and news. Library staff with a strong grounding in disability issues will be able to speak knowledgeably and actively participate in casual conversations with patrons and colleagues when these topics arise. Time spent expanding your capacity for understanding or empathy for persons with disabilities is never wasted.

## Demographics of Your User Community

Information about your user community can be helpful when planning library services, especially for people with disabilities. Demographic information about the inhabitants and organization of your town, school, or region can be obtained from the websites of local government or organizations, as well as through state and national initiatives that utilize data that has already been collected. For example, when you are seeking information about the age ranges of all of your possible library users, your local health department or school district may have already compiled some of the information you need. Sources include your local or state government, as well as third parties who have done the same research, including new businesses, real estate brokers, or other offices that also need these figures for similar purposes.

And, of course, census and other federal government data will provide many details, down to the town and county level. Socioeconomic information may also be useful when planning library services of all kinds. This includes data on income, health status, housing, education levels, and the like. These data points can help identify some of your community's needs and characteristics, such as health care trends or shifting wealth or population averages, as well as help to point to trends over time.

Some libraries and universities compile databases that aggregate this type of information from a variety of sources like the US Census Bureau, the Internal Revenue Services, and the Social Security Administration. For example, they may contain information about the levels of employment and unemployment of people with disabilities in your area, or where various nonprofit agencies are located. You may even be able to analyze this information on an interactive map.

Additional variables like consumer spending patterns and preferences, the prevalence of wireless Internet access, and other types of consumer life-

 **For Your Information**

Sources of data about your local constituents:

- Government (local, state, national publications, documents, etc.)
- Media (television, radio, newspapers, etc.)
- Websites (public, private, social networks, etc.)
- Business and financial records, corporate filings
- Real estate records
- Labor unions and trade and professional associations
- Business associations (Chambers of Commerce, development centers, etc.)
- Educational institutions
- Existing market research studies or commercial reports

style information are available. Some sources are free from public research organizations like RAND and the Pew Internet Research Center, or from government-sponsored surveys like the Consumer Expenditure Survey from the Bureau of Labor Statistics.

Licensed library databases often aggregate this information and provide useful dashboards for comparing multiple types of information for a specific geographic area. Databases from vendors like ReferenceUSA, PolicyMap, or Data-Planet can help create data "mashups" from multiple sources, or pinpoint selected data in counties or census tracts via Geographical Information System (GIS) features.

## Social Media and Online Communities

Social media is another way to research the interests, characteristics, and trends of your local community. Checking to see who has made your library's web page a favorite on Facebook, or what other web pages are important to users who also enjoy libraries, can reveal valuable information that has been willingly volunteered by members of your community. Your users' public online profiles may also reveal information about their interests and people they know or admire. Even if libraries mined just part of this existing public data, they stand to learn quite a bit about the interests of members of their patrons.

In "Communities of Participation: A Comparison of Disability and Aging Identified Groups on Facebook and LinkedIn" (2013), authors Paul M. Baker, John C. Bricout, Nathan W. Moon, Barry Coughlan, and Jessica Pater looked at the online mobility limitations of older individuals and individuals with disabilities. They reported that both groups exhibit similar patterns of increased online interactions via social media sites such as Facebook and LinkedIn. These results suggest that libraries should add online resources to their social media sites, including links to news and events in the community. It becomes essential for libraries, businesses, community organizations, and municipal agencies to keep their social media sites up-to-date, interesting, and accessible. Social media is an integral part of your outreach strategy to stay connected with all users in the community.

In addition, users of LinkedIn and other professional social network sites voluntarily post biographical information (e.g., which schools they attended

---

✓ **Checklist**

Investigate these types of social media opportunities:

- ☐ Social networking sites
- ☐ Micro-news and micro-blog sites
- ☐ Photo and video sharing
- ☐ Website blogging tools
- ☐ Wiki collaboration tools
- ☐ Rating and review sites
- ☐ Location-based meet-up tools
- ☐ Virtual worlds and online games

---

or where they live). More and more people now volunteer information about themselves on social media sites, and this information can be found via keywords typed into search engines. Use these tools to help your library connect with new or current patrons.

Some online communities identify with disabilities very specifically, such as Disability Scoop, an online news site and blog that has tens of thousands of followers on Facebook. Other online communities are valued by users specifically because they do not disclose disabilities of their members. Therefore, approaching new social networks with care will help you understand users' motives for participation and their norms for sharing information.

Other online groups will disclose their affiliations, funding, advocacy goals, or other specifics, so it is important to review all of these aspects before recommending or linking to any online communities. In addition, social groups and websites from other countries can provide interesting perspectives and innovative ideas from which to draw inspiration for your own programs and services.

There are so many online social networking sites, and so many existing and emerging online tools to help facilitate connections between people who share similar interests to list here. However, talking to people of all ages about what services they currently use is an excellent way to find out where your users are before designing strategies to market library services there.

## Library Science and Disability Studies Literature

Checking general article databases such as those from EBSCO or ProQuest, as well as specialized databases of library literature and education literature, is a good first step. When searching, use keywords as well as subject headings, which do not remain standard over time and thus may reduce the number of search results. The search terms *disab\** or *disabil?* are truncated words that will return article keywords such as disability (singular), disabilities (plural), and disabled (an adjective). Check each database's search tips page for an indication of whether truncation is offered and what particular wildcard characters should be used. Also check for suggested similar terms or thesaurus entries if those features are available.

Searching subject headings in the main search query with additional keywords will provide the most targeted results. Library of Congress, Sears, or MeSH subject headings will change with time, and new ones are continually added by professional catalogers when the amount of literature collected on a topic or activity warrants it, or the language has evolved sufficiently to prompt a change.

There are literally hundreds of subject headings related to disabilities and their related terms. The National Library Service provides a list of relevant "see" and "see also" references.

---

 **For Your Information**

Some of the many Library of Congress Subject Headings related to disabilities:

- Disabilities
- People with disabilities
- [profession or identity group] with disabilities (e.g., athletes with disabilities, students with disabilities)
- Disability awareness
- Disability studies
- Disabled veterans
- Discrimination against people with disabilities
- [type of] disability (e.g., developmental disabilities, learning disabilities)
- [type of] disorder (e.g., movement disorders, perceptual disorders)
- [name of the condition] (e.g., deafness, Asperger syndrome)

Pathfinders, bibliographies, webliographies, guides, indexes, and hand-books will also have excellent information on best practice literature. Resource materials of these types will help to list, sort, and rank the disability studies literature to help determine its relative importance, popularity, or citation patterns. Google Scholar and many other databases also feature a "cited by" function, which will help to locate articles on similar topics that referenced each other for background information. Linked data initiatives will also improve access to materials on these subjects in the future.

Some of these resource lists are prepared by leading library and educational organizations, making both current and archived lists useful for collection purposes. The Schneider Family Book Award administered by the American Library Association is an example of a booklist that can be used for collection development and current awareness. The award honors an author or illustra-

---

 **For Your Information**

**Here are some winners of the Schneider Family Book Awards given by ALA for authentic portrayals of the disability experience:**

Abeel, Samantha. *My Thirteenth Winter: A Memoir.* Orchard, 2003.

Baskin, Nora Raleigh. *Anything but Typical.* Simon and Schuster, 2009.

Chaconas, Dori. *Dancing with Katya.* Peachtree, 2006.

Dwight, Laura. *Brothers and Sisters.* Star Bright Books, 2005.

Finke, Beth. *Hanni and Beth: Safe and Sound.* Blue Marlin, 2007.

Herrera, Juan Felipe. *Featherless/Desplumado: Story/Cuento.* Children's Book Press, 2004.

Hunt, Lynda Mullaly. *Fish in a Tree.* Nancy Paulsen Books, Penguin Group, 2015.

Lord, Cynthia. *Rules.* Scholastic Press, 2006.

Mazer, Harry, and Peter Lerangis. *Somebody, Please Tell Me Who I Am.* Simon and Schuster, 2012.

Nuzum, K. A. *A Small White Scar.* Joanna Cotler Books, 2006.

Seeger, Pete and Paul DuBois Jacobs. *The Deaf Musicians.* Putnam's, 2006.

Toten, Teresa. *The Unlikely Hero of Room 13B.* Delacorte Press, Penguin Random House, 2013.

tor for a book that "embodies an artistic expression of the disability experience for child and adolescent audiences."

In library catalogs such as WorldCat, you will find secondary places to look for gray literature like conference proceedings and white papers. Resources like position statements, speeches, or testimonies before Congress can be found via your favorite search engine, on other libraries' research guides, or via federated search tools.

Many databases will let you set an alert for new journal articles, and many library systems will allow you to request notification when new books on a particular topic arrive. If you notice that your local library does not have enough materials on disability topics, request them through interlibrary loan, or suggest some particular items for purchase to your local librarians.

Casting a wide net when searching will help you to develop a robust search strategy. So many different resources around the web, around the country, and around the world are excellent sources of information about disability trends, legislation, and best practices.

Keep an open mind when seeking ideas, yet double-check your favorite materials for their biases and what your selections may reveal about your own. Investigate funding sources or political agendas of organizations or authors in order to seek balance.

## Professional Communities

Professional associations, organizations, and groups contribute significant knowledge and insights to the profession of librarianship and the entire field of education. Professional communities both inside and outside of the library world are a continual supply of current information.

LISTSERV® communications are still important in librarianship, and yes, they're still going strong. Signing up for one of these e-mail alerts or discussion services ensures that disabilities topics are brought to your attention regularly. For example, DSSHEL, the Disabled Student Services in Higher Education electronic mailing list from the University of Buffalo, is a forum for higher education professionals involved in the delivery of services to students with disabilities.

Informal online discussions often reveal different perspectives and emerging practices, and do so faster than any book or article. Some professional

**For Your Information**

Types of information provided by professional electronic mailing lists:

- Current happenings in the discipline
- Grant opportunities announcements
- Surveys and their results
- Networks of professionals in your industry
- Questions and answers about difficult issues
- Government advocacy initiatives
- New resources and services
- Special interest group or task force invitations
- News, current legal issues, and media reports
- Workshops, webinars, and websites

organizations restrict their online mailing list discussions solely to members, but others allow anyone to sign up. A quick search engine query of disabilities LISTSERV®s will provide the most recent results about what groups are available. Remember, some groups are specifically for disabled users themselves, so research the communities you are interested in before joining.

Examples of professional organizations that provide electronic mailing lists are abundant. The Association on Higher Education and Disability (AHEAD), is another active group that supports full participation of persons with disabilities in postsecondary education; the National Association of State Directors of Special Education (NASDSE) has announcement groups and posts information about events; and the Council for Exceptional Children (CEC) discusses ways to improve educational outcomes for individuals with exceptionalities.

You probably already know about Recording for the Blind and Dyslexic (RFB&D), a national nonprofit that utilizes volunteers to read textbooks for those who cannot read standard print. A variety of other communities provide awareness in unique ways, as well as opportunities to participate. For example, Syracuse University hosts an Imaging Disability in Film Series each year, in which it honors films and their creators for avoiding stereotypes and appropriately depicting characters with disabilities.

Educational associations will also have cooperative groups that rally multiple stakeholders to promote advocacy and constant quality improvement of our systems and organizations. Two examples are the National Joint Committee on Learning Disabilities (NJCLD), which gathers representatives of organi-

**For Your Information**

Follow the news and activities of these resource organizations to uncover new ideas:

- Administration for Community Living (www.acl.gov)
- Administration on Intellectual and Developmental Disabilities (www.acl.gov/Programs/AIDD/Index.aspx)
- Association of University Centers on Disabilities (www.aucd.org)
- Intellectual and Developmental Disability Research Center (www.bcm .edu/research/centers/intellectual-developmental-disabilities)
- Leadership Education in Neurodevelopmental Disabilities Programs (https://www.aucd.org/template/page.cfm?id=473)
- Maternal and Child Health Bureau (http://mchb.hrsa.gov)
- National Association of the Deaf (www.nad.org)
- National Federation of the Blind (www.nfd.org)
- National Institute for Child Health and Development (www.nichd.nih.gov)
- National Institute on Disability, Independent Living, and Rehabilitation Research (www.acl.gov/programs/NIDILRR)
- US Department of Health and Human Services (www.hhs.gov)

zations committed to the education and welfare of individuals with learning disabilities; and the Association of Specialized and Cooperative Library Agencies (ASCLA), a division of ALA that strives to improve the quality of library services for people with special needs, including those with disabilities.

Universities also may be affiliated with research centers that design empirical studies and lend expertise and advocacy. For example, the Technology Access Program (TAP) is one of Gallaudet University's research centers. The center is comprised of faculty affiliated with different departments and programs, and strives to advance communication technologies for people with disabilities.

Foundations and advocacy groups, as well as local nonprofit organizations, are all excellent sources of information about work on disabilities issues in your local area and around the country. Very often, these groups award grants to institutions for innovative projects that serve persons with disabilities, and they are excellent sources of current information. Joining their mailing lists and checking their websites regularly will keep you informed of new opportunities to partner or apply for grant funding. State libraries may help their librarians to make additional connections to these types of organizations in your region.

---

### ✔ Checklist

Strategies for finding information from potential partner organizations:

- ☐ Contact job service or workforce employment centers.
- ☐ Explore college and university career centers.
- ☐ Partner with disability-related advocacy organizations.
- ☐ Ask for referrals of people with disabilities who are available to consult on planning.
- ☐ Browse or search for disability-related publications.
- ☐ Investigate disability-related websites.
- ☐ Host tables at disability-related job fairs.
- ☐ Exchange bulletin board postings with vocational rehabilitation centers.
- ☐ Establish summer internship and mentoring programs.
- ☐ Connect with independent living centers.

---

In fact, agencies that fund many major grants, especially those that provide funding to serve people with disabilities, will rely on your analysis of how potential or projected library services will meet the needs of users in your community. E-mail lists about grants, along with links to the professional or advocacy organizations that sponsor them, are useful awareness tools that will be periodically delivered to your inbox upon subscription.

Organizations that specialize in other disciplines are also good sources of information. For example, the National Endowment for the Arts (NEA) has an excellent "Step-by-Step Guide to Accessible Cultural Programs and Organizations," which relates to libraries of multiple types, not just those organizations who run arts programs. These types of resources are quite detailed, and new information can be found year-round. In addition, these new sources will inform any strategic planning effort towards an inclusive library environment.

As you can see, much of the information provided about hosting events, hiring workers, creating library programming, or simply creating a comfortable atmosphere can be cross-applied easily to the process of planning inclusive environments and services for people with disabilities. Good ideas do not always have to be specifically targeted toward libraries, but can be used to improve the experiences of all library users.

## Internships, Mentoring, and Volunteers

Another source of essential up-to-date information is your local library school. Consider hosting internships for those studying to be librarians, or offering mentoring to new librarians. Current students who are working in your library or who are volunteering for on-the-job experience are invaluable sources of current awareness. One particular value of partnerships with university library and information services programs is access to a steady stream of new information and methods, as well as the confirmation of existing practices that flow from those currently enrolled in librarianship courses.

Benefits gained from internships can prove invaluable for college students who want to strengthen their resumes with practical experience related to their career goals. Libraries can provide college students with internship opportunities in various majors and areas of concentration such as computer science, English, graphic arts, marketing, and public relations.

Consider tailoring an intern's experience to specific duties and tasks that will enhance and improve the inclusiveness of your library environment. To further improve accessibility, seek out interns with disabilities who may have additional perspectives that could truly benefit your library operations. In this way, you will have exponentially increased staff time spent on disabilities issues. A student intern who is a computer science major and who also is blind or has a visual impairment would be invaluable for reviewing and critiquing your website and web pages. By using the WCAG 2.0 guidelines, the student can provide immediate feedback and recommendations to improve your website.

The availability of work-study students on college campuses gives libraries another valuable resource to promote a user-centered culture. Hiring students with disabilities will help you to develop a library environment where all staff members are actively involved in the training and mentoring of students and at the same time gaining a better understanding of an intern's disability.

## Materials from Government and Advocacy Groups

There are far too many organizations whose missions include disabilities advocacy than could ever be listed here. Nevertheless, a few examples may help to determine the range of free resources and information available. Both public and private sources can provide insights on new ways to think about disability services.

Disability.gov is considered the premier source for information on disability issues, services, and content provided by the US federal government. It contains useful blogs highlighting resources and services, as well as a comprehensive list of links on all types of disability topics. The site also connects to additional federal agencies that are involved with disabilities issues.

The US Architectural and Transportation Barriers Compliance Board, also called the US Access Board, is another federal agency that promotes equality for people with disabilities. Libraries will be interested in their suggestions for dimensions of aisles and shelving, as well as many other accessible design recommendations. This organization focuses on the development of accessibility guidelines and standards for both exterior and interior facilities.

The ADA National Network has ten regional centers around the United States. It provides information, guidance, and online training on the Americans with Disabilities Act to users from all types of organizations. Librarians will also want to check search engine tools like Google's advanced search operators to find additional websites, library guides, or resource lists that point to this and other suggested URLs.

Each presidential administration usually posts a website discussing its agenda for disabilities legislation, executive orders and issues of concern, and topics ranging from health care and civil rights to employment and technology. Many similar websites will track proposed legislation in Congress, and post outcomes as they occur. Professional electronic mailing lists will also provide this service and often identify opportunities to write to your elected representatives to ask for their support.

The National Council on Disability maintains an annual list of publication and policy briefs that highlight important issues for people with disabilities, including access, full participation, and other topics. As an independent federal agency, it makes recommendations to various government branches that affect over 50 million Americans with disabilities.

Pepnet2, for example, is a federally funded project that offers free and self-paced online training modules about accommodations, as well as many tip sheets and resources. Tip sheets from this and other organizations can be extremely useful for staff training as well as for promoting awareness among library patrons and your entire community. Also consider researching the websites of these organizations' counterparts in other countries for more ideas, practices, and guidelines.

**For Your Information**

Other government agencies with free resources and information:
- Department of Education (DOE)
- Department of Health and Human Services
- Department of Housing and Urban Development
- Department of Justice ADA homepage
- Department of Labor (FMLA regulations)
- Department of Transportation (DOT)
- Equal Employment Opportunity Commission (EEOC)
- Federal Communications Commission (FCC) Disabilities Issues Task Force
- Internal Revenue Service (IRS) Surveys and Reports
- National Institute on Disability and Rehabilitation Research (NIDRR)
- President's Committee on Employment of People with Disabilities
- Small Business Administration
- Social Security Administration
- US Government Printing Office's Searchable Federal Register

The Job Accommodation Network, a service of the Office of Disability Employment Policy and the United States Department of Labor, provides free confidential technical assistance about disability accommodations in the workplace. This site can be used by both employees and employers, and it serves as a clearinghouse of best practices and options to accommodate all types of disabilities.

The Great Lakes ADA Center is another group that works with other centers, individuals, committees, and like-minded disability organizations to host free webinars and business events, in addition to distributing resource packets and other materials. It efficiently responds to queries, whether from government entities (federal, state, local) or other interested parties. Many other groups are willing and available to answer questions, to set up training, or to provide referral information once you contact them to express your needs.

## Conducting Needs Assessments, Surveys, and Polls

Sometimes, you will need information that goes beyond what you've found through a literature search or by questioning your colleagues at peer institutions. Often you'll need more specific information about your community of current and potential users. This is an indication that it is time to do your own empirical research.

Literature searches that include the words "method" or "survey" or "questionnaire," along with keywords or subject headings describing the topic at hand, will yield studies and experiments that have already been conducted and critiqued. It is important to use both professional library literature as well as nonprofit research as the basis on which to build your own study design.

To find emerging research, look for databases that include dissertations and theses from the library catalogs of local universities or their open-source database counterparts, as well as national dissertation databases such as those available through ProQuest. These will provide an idea of what topics are currently being researched and how people are going about collecting data on these topics.

Libraries can learn a great deal by conducting primary research both before and after initiatives are implemented. Indeed, librarians can conduct empirical research at any time in order to find out how things are going on their project or how their library measures up to others. Especially during times of complacency, it can be important to pinpoint why things seem to be going well, rather than only investigating problems.

Evaluations done with a more rigorous eye to social science research design—qualitative, quantitative, or mixed methods—will make your assessments more systematic. When it's time to do your own survey, needs assessment, or study, library resources will help you learn about the appropriate ways to conduct rigorous analysis of a particular area of your library. Remember to use both "how-to" materials as well as other people's research articles as examples.

 **For Your Information**

Research methods to choose when designing your own empirical research:

- Surveys or questionnaires
- Interviews
- Focus groups
- Case studies
- Ethnography
- Document analysis
- Naturalistic observations
- Experimental study
- Quasi-experimental study
- Mixed methods or multi-method
- Correlation and regression analysis
- Meta-analysis

You will also need to determine the purpose for conducting primary research (as opposed to the secondary research we all perform regularly when we search previous studies of others). You may just be exploring an idea or connection, or you may be looking for a solution and evaluating different approaches to determine which are effective. You may even be searching for ways to support one side of an argument or another. Objectivity and sound research design choices will ensure that your results are taken seriously.

Helping your library staff members to stay current will also help your organization become more nimble when responding to challenges or introducing new services. Current awareness need not be merely a habit of mind for individuals, but also a habit of practice for your organization. Making time to regularly read through many of the materials that we order, recommend, or promote will help us to remain up-to-date easily with each successive effort.

## Resources

American Association of People with Disabilities. "Announcing the Disability Download!" www.aapd.com/resources/press-room/disabilitydownload.html.

American Library Association. "Schneider Family Book Award [current year]." www.ala.org/awardsgrants/schneider-family-book-award.

American Library Association. "Schneider Family Book Award [all years]." www.ala .org/awardsgrants/awards/1/all_years.

American Library Association. "Select Bibliography of Children's Books about the Disability Experience." www.ala.org/awardsgrants/sites/ala.org.awards grants/files/content/awardsrecords/schneideraward/2009_schneider_bio _children.pdf.

Americans with Disabilities Act National Network. "Information, Guidance, and Training on the Americans with Disabilities Act." http://adata.org.

Baker, Paul M. A., John C. Bricout, Nathan W. Moon, Barry Coughlan, and Jessica Pater. 2013. "Communities of Participation: A Comparison of Disability and Aging Identified Groups on Facebook and LinkedIn." *Telematics and Informatics* 30 (1): 22–34.

Disabled World. "Disability News and Information." www.disabled-world.com.

Guerra, Francesca. 2010. "Simplifying Access: Metadata for Medieval Disability Studies." *PNLA Quarterly* 74 (2): 10–26.

HEATH Resource Center at the National Youth Transitions Center, George Washington University. "Guidance and Career Counselors' Toolkit: Advising High School Students with Disabilities on Postsecondary Options." https://heath.gwu.edu/sites/heath.gwu.edu/files/downloads/Toolkit%202014.pdf.

Hill, Heather. 2013. "Disability and Accessibility in the Library and Information Science Literature: A Content Analysis." *Library and Information Science Research* 35 (2): 137–42.

Holmes, Jennifer L. 2008. "Patrons with Developmental Disabilities: A Needs Assessment Survey." *New Library World* 109 (11/12): 533–45.

Job Accommodation Network. "JAN: For Employers." https://askjan.org/empl.

Library of Congress, National Library Service. "NLS: That All May Read: Subject Headings Used in the NLS Reference Collections on Visual and Physical Disabilities." www.loc.gov/nls/reference/subjectheadings.html.

Mason, Karen. 2010. "Disability Studies: Online Resources for a Growing Discipline." *College and Research Libraries News* 71 (5): 252–60.

National Council on Disability. "Publications and Policy Briefs." www.ncd.gov/publications.

National Endowment for the Arts. "Accessibility Planning and Resource Guide for Cultural Administrators." https://www.arts.gov/accessibility/accessibility-resources/publications-checklists/accessibility-planning-and-resource and https://www.arts.gov/sites/default/files/AccessibilityPlanningAll.pdf.

Nganji, Julius T., Mike Brayshaw, and Brian Tompsett. 2012. "Ontology-Driven Disability-Aware e-Learning Personalisation with ONTODAPS." *Campus-Wide Information Systems* 30 (1): 17–34.

Pepnet2. "Serving Disability Services Professionals." http://pepnet.org.

Rivas-Costa, Carlos, Luis Anido-Rifon, Manuel J. Fernandez-Iglesias, Miguel A. Gomez-Carballa, Sonia Valladares-Rodriguez, and Roberto Soto-Barreiros. 2014. "An Accessible Platform for People with Disabilities." *International Journal of Human-Computer Interaction* 30 (6): 480–94.

Subramaniam, Mega M., Howard Rodriguez-Mori, Paul T. Jaeger, and Renee Franklin Hill. 2012. "The Implications of a Decade of Diversity-Related Doctoral Dissertations (2000–2009) in LIS: Supporting Inclusive Library Practices." *The Library Quarterly* 82 (3): 361–77.

Trevisan, Filippo. 2013. "Disability and New Media." *Information, Communication and Society* 16 (10): 1697–99.

United States Access Board. "U.S. Access Board: Advancing Full Access and Inclusion for All." https://www.access-board.gov.

United States Department of Labor. Office of Disability Employment Policy. "Disability.gov." https://www.disability.gov/what-does-disability-gov-do.

———. "Employer Perspectives on Employment of People with Disabilities." www.dol.gov/odep/documents/employerperspectives.pdf.

United States Government. The White House. "Issues: Disabilities." https://www.whitehouse.gov/issues/disabilities.

# about the authors

**MICHELLE KOWALSKY** is a librarian and professor at Rowan University, Glassboro, New Jersey. She teaches and supervises undergraduate learners and graduate students in their research endeavors. Michelle holds an EdD from Pepperdine University and an MLS from Rutgers University, and is a National Board Certified Teacher of Library Media. Her most recent activities have been upgrade of Campbell Library's Digital Learning Center with software and furniture recommended by students with disabilities; development of information literacy instruction and reference services in a variety of subject areas, most recently for business majors; and supervision of dissertation research for doctoral students in the College of Education. Prior to working in academia, Michelle worked as a public librarian, a corporate librarian, and a K–12 school librarian and teacher for over twenty years.

**JOHN WOODRUFF** is Director of the Academic Success Center and Disability Resources at Rowan University, Glassboro, New Jersey. He coordinates campus services for students with disabilities and manages transitions for students entering college. John holds an MS in Health Education from St. Joseph's University and a BS in Business Administration from St. Francis University (Loretto, Pennsylvania). His most recent activities include outreach to faculty and students to increase empathy for the varying needs of students; development of year-round speaker programs, activities, and events to promote understanding on campus and in the local community; and leadership of faculty-led and community-led strategic partnerships for awareness, training, and mentoring. John's professional career reflects over thirty years of education, training, administration, and management of employment and training programs for persons with disabilities.

# index